Craft Floor Malting: A Practical Guide

by Gabe Toth

Copyright 2019 © Gabe Toth

ISBN 978-1-7322354-1-0

White Mule Press a division of the
American Distilling Institute
PO Box 577
Hayward, CA 94541
whitemulepress.com

Photographs by Andrew Faulkner and Gabe Toth;
and courtesy of Warminster Malting and Dave Thomas

① Farm:
Growing 2 row barley
- 6 months-
Harvesting
- 1 day-

② Cleaning
grain of
chaff
-3 hours-

③ Steeping
2-3 days

STEEP
TANK

④ Rake the malt
-Twice a day for
5 days-

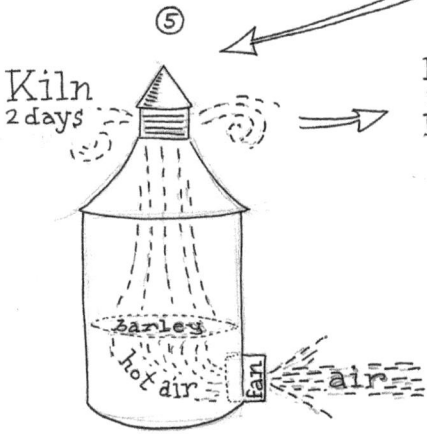

⑤ Kiln
2 days

barley
hot air fan air

⑥ Distilling
in a copper
pot still

⑦ Barreling -1 to 5 years in
charred American "alba" Oak
(alba gives notes of vanilla to whiskey)

Illustration © Michael R. Hall

Acknowledgments

I have to thank my partner Stefanie first and foremost for her support and for understanding, as much as is possible, why I would spend so much time locked in the basement working on a fairly esoteric topic.

The work done by the Craft Maltsters Guild has been an invaluable resource, and the help of Adam Paul from Integrated Process Engineers & Constructors (IPEC) was a lifesaver.

Many thanks also to malt guru Dave Thomas for his assistance in fact-checking and content suggestions, and to Bill Owens, Andrew Faulkner, Matt Kramer and Gail Sands for assembling this work into its final form. Without the support of the staff at the American Distilling Institute, this project could never have come together.

A special thanks to Chris Garratt of Warminster Maltings and Rob Moody of Crisp Malting, who opened their archives to provide some beautiful historic images, as well as a depth of understanding that only comes with more than a century of institutional knowledge.

Finally, a heartfelt thank-you to all of the craft maltsters who took the time to speak to me for this project. Through their generosity, they've painted a much more detailed picture of their world than I ever could have.

Table of Contents

Introduction / 3

Resources / 119

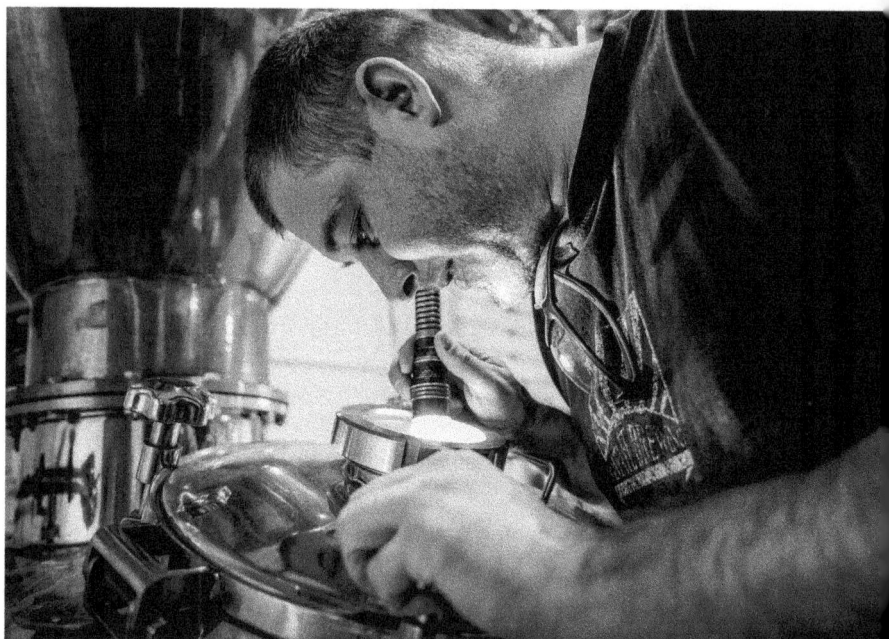

Flashlight in hand, author Gabe Toth looks into the still at The Family Jones Distllery.

Introduction

When I started this project, I was running the brewhouse at a small brewpub in Boulder, CO. I was the type of brewer that Ron Silberstein of Admiral Maltings describes in Chapter 7, who uses specialty malt, barrels and — especially — boatloads of hops to bring flavor to beer. Having worked in both the brewing and distilling industries for the past several years, I had a certain respect for finely crafted malts, such as English floor malt as the base of an amber or premium German pilsner malt in a crisp lager. But they had very specific roles. For most of my beers, commodity malt — a standardized, mostly interchangeable starch source — would comprise 90 percent or more of the raw goods.

To move beyond that mind-set requires that we move beyond commodity malt. As a crop that prefers cold, dry climates, most U.S. barley is grown in a swath of land that extends from Washington and Oregon, through Montana and Idaho, to North Dakota and Minnesota. Because of transport costs, commodity maltsters such as Briess (Wisconsin), Great Western (Washington) and Rahr (Minnesota) will set up in or near those areas. But barley was once grown all over the country.

The designers of the California Building in San Diego, built for the Panama-California Exposition in 1915, quoted from Deuteronomy in black-and-white tiles, "Terram Frumenti Hordei, ac Vinarum, in qua Ficus et Malogranata et Oliveta Nascuntur, Terram Olei ac Mellis," or "A land of wheat and barley and vines... a land of olive oil and honey." In places like upstate New York, farmers are reclaiming that history and trying to grow malting barley again. Maltsters like Barn Owl Malt in Canada and Warminster Maltings in England offer distillers and brewers the opportunity to reconnect with their regional agriculture and use malt that was specifically grown near them.

As barley becomes more local, it increases the opportunities to localize malt production. A brewer or distiller who can access local barley can take greater control of the supply chain with a malthouse, and the advent of farm breweries and farm distilleries provides a ready-made opportunity for on-site malting. Like many small maltsters, the Leopold Bros. distillery in Denver uses grain grown within a few hours of them — in Longmont and the San Luis Valley — to fill their two 5,000-pound steeps.

Growing and malting one's own barley, or working directly with local farmers who can provide malting barley, also creates the opportunity to find unique heritage or heirloom varieties, grains that provide something not measurable in a malt analysis. At Crisp Malting, they've brought back into production the first ever selected malting barley, Chevallier. It was first isolated in 1824 and lasted for about a hundred years before being supplanted by other varieties. "Historically, most of the floor maltings would have been working with that. It pretty well dominated all the way through," according to Rob Moody, Director of Group Logistics and Craft Brewing at Crisp.

Crisp acquired seeds from a bank and was able to revive the line, growing a barley that has "a really punchy, robust malt flavor to it," he said. "People have been raving about it here, when they do old-style brews particularly. It's amazing stuff. If you put four base malts together that all look exactly the same on paper, if you taste them side by side, they taste completely different. It's been a revelation to us."

There are thousands of barley varieties in the world. Less than one percent are appropriate for malting, and an even smaller number are currently seeing much use. Older breeds can be more flavorful, but they come with their own agronomic challenges. Chevallier has a long straw compared to modern varieties, making it prone to falling over easily. It also reflects the time that it comes from, in its own unique way. "It seems to be a real nitrogen-scavenging variety, which makes sense," Moody said. "I suppose back then they wouldn't have had a lot of fertilizer."

Even working with standard varieties, though, floor malting offers a tangible flavor difference from drum- or box-malting systems. In a presentation to the American Society of Brewing Chemists Malt Flavor and Aroma Symposium, David Griggs of Crisp showed that malt produced in their floor-malting facility versus two of their automated maltings had different relative levels of volatile compounds and, in some cases, contained compounds that were not present in malt from the automated systems.

Griggs said the full significance of his findings was yet to be determined, given that flavor threshold would impact how these

Rick Wasmund at the Copper Fox Distillery, formally the Lord Paget Inn, rakes the malt.

individual compounds would contribute to the overall perception of flavor and aroma, but his results affirm the subjective opinions of brewers over many years that floor malt is qualitatively different from pneumatic malt.

Nonetheless, since Alphonse Saladin created his malting box in 1883, improving on his mentor Nicholas Galland's pneumatic germination box by adding vertical screw turners, floor malting has been yielding market share. Moody spent the first 10 years of his career as a floor maltster for Guinness, as his father did, before the brewery shut down its three English floor-malting locations and moved production to a modern plant in 1994.

Recently, though, craft maltsters have found floor malting to be a more cost-effective way of entering the market. In 2012 when there were 33 breweries in Maine, Blue Ox Malthouse founder Joel Alex found himself talking to a craft brewer about barley being farmed nearby and interest in using locally grown ingredients, "but that processing capacity was missing," he said.

Grain that was grown in Maine was generally exported to Canada for processing, and local brewers had to buy it back through an importer in New York. Alex started researching and became excited about the opportunity, turning down an opportunity to go to grad school in favor of opening a malthouse in Lisbom Falls, Maine.

"I saw the time was now, people were ready for a locally sourced and malted grain," he said. He received a couple of grants to research and learn about malting, brought on a partner in 2014 and by October 2015 had jumped from pilot maltings of 100 to 400 pounds right up to 10,000 pounds.

While turnkey box-malting systems are more expensive to establish than floor malting, at the time they weren't even available at the five-ton scale. He found that floor malting required the lowest (but still significant) capital investment costs and fit in with what brewers around him were producing. "They're doing a lot of traditional styles. This is traditional, handcrafted malt," Alex said. "Every single day we shovel, we interact with our grain. It's traditionally crafted malt for traditionally crafted beer.

"We've really shown that floor malting is a great way to not only highlight our local grain, but also produce high quality, consistent products for our customers," he said. It's also a way to be a greater part of the community. In addition to reclaiming that value-added processing for his city and state, floor malting gives Alex the opportunity to employ residents and provide them with a living wage. "I could spend six figures on a piece of equipment that could mechanize everything or I could provide a good, quality job for my community," he said.

Malting is a biological process, and this manual is not intended as a recipe book or chemistry textbook. It is meant as a practical guide, a starting point, for the distiller or brewer who wants to take more control of the supply chain and reconnect with the agricultural aspect of their work. There are guidelines included, but they are not recipes. "There's no simple answer in malting," Alex said. "It's really about how well you understand the process behind it and the theory and the relationships."

Malting does not have to be complicated, nor does it absolutely require expensive and sophisticated equipment. Mark Watkins, owner of Mt. Uncle Distillery in Queensland, Australia, buys a 350-pound sack of barley from a cousin who farms it. He'll pour the barley out on the floor of a shed and soak it with a garden hose, then cover it with bags to prevent it from drying out. Three to four times a day he'll uncover the barley, rake it and water it again. After three days the barley will have sprouted, and he'll water one more day and continue raking for a few more days. The grain will be moved outside and spread on a black plastic sheet to dry in the sun. Raking knocks off most of the culms, and the dried malt is ready to be milled, mashed, fermented and distilled.

There are many variables to floor malting, and many avenues to get to quality malt. There is no one-size-fits-all recipe to making good malt, the best answer will be the one that best suits your space, budget and other local factors. To that end, we've included stories and suggestions from some very generous maltsters in the United States, Canada and England. Think about what they're doing and take what works for your circumstances.

Water drops into the grain in the custom-built
soaking tank at Stoutridge Vineyard & Distillery.

Chapter One

Steeping

Steeping is the linchpin of quality malt production. The steeping barley will set the stage for the speed and quality of modification, directly impacting the quality of the final product.

The goal of steeping is to increase the moisture content of barley from a post-harvest storage moisture content of about 12% up to 42–46% to encourage germination. More than a century ago, a batch of barley would be steeped at 55–60°F for two to three days, but sometimes up to six days, though the danger of drowning the barley was already known and the steep water would be changed periodically to try to introduce air.

In a modern malthouse, hydration is usually undertaken over the same amount of time, but using alternating soaking periods and air rests. Crisp uses a fairly standard steep schedule, with an initial six-hour steep, a 12- to 16-hour air rest, another six hours wet, 12–16 hours dry, a couple of hours for a third steep and then a four-hour air rest before casting, according to Rob Moody.

"You really want to get it on the floor and have it ready to go," he said. "As soon as you get enough moisture into the grain and then you give it an air rest, you want it to start chitting, you want it to start to germinate."

Joel Alex cautioned against relying too heavily on schedules and times, but rather encouraged monitoring moisture content. "It's not just a time and temperature thing, it's more of a moisture and temperature," he said. "If you can control your moisture well enough, then you can set timetables."

Devin Huffman at Barn Owl Malt in Ontario emphasized the importance of not over-steeping or under-steeping. Moisture can't be taken out of the malt if it's over-steeped, and once germination starts, the barley won't use additional moisture to properly modify, but will instead start going to shoot too quickly.

"It seems like it should be a fairly straightforward part of the process — just get it wet and get it germinating —but if you over- or under-steep it by a couple of percentage points, the behavior during germination is dramatically different," he said. "To a certain extent, you can push it one way or the other by adjusting the steep-out moisture, which is why the steep schedule and the consistent steep-out moistures for your grain lot are so critical. The end product can be quite dramatically changed if you're not watching it, if you're not hydrating it very precisely every time."

Even processing from the same grain lot will change over the course of the year. The grain itself will evolve, and ambient conditions will require changes to the way it's handled. Because Huffman doesn't need to run the air-conditioning in the malthouse during the winter, he's not stripping as much moisture out during flooring and the green malt is less prone to excessive drying

"In winter, the ambient air in the malthouse is usually saturated, and we end up having to run dehumidifiers," he said. "[The grain] needs a little bit of evaporation throughout the process. We budget a certain percent moisture loss per day and then we try to manage the humidity in the malthouse to accommodate that. There's such a wide difference in relative humidity between the peak of summer and the coldest days of winter, we often have to modify the steep schedule a little bit just to accommodate."

To determine his steep schedule, Huffman does small-scale testing, micro-malting about five pounds and checking it on the moisture balance, before working with a new lot of barley and on regular intervals to adjust for seasonal variations in a lot he is working with. Germination can be adjusted on the fly, as long as a little extra time is built into the schedule. "But," Huffman said, "if you don't know what the grain's water uptake profile is like, you will have few options to correct and recover a piece once it's been wetted.

"So for every grain lot that we're working with, we develop a unique steeping profile. When we're developing a steep schedule, we usually design it for around 45, 46 percent, but then once we start germinating those grains, if they're not performing well, if it's germinating too aggressively and putting on too much rootlet growth which then translates to losses, we might scale it back a little bit. Or if the barley is tough and slow to modify, we can help it by pushing the moisture up."

The difference in water uptake can be enormous. He said barley from 2016, a drought year, would take 27 hours of total immersion time to reach the target moisture level, whereas the same variety from the same farm in 2017, a wet growing season, would reach steep-out moisture in 12 or 13 hours.

At Warminster Maltings, Managing Director and Head Maltster Chris Garratt also relies on testing for germination energy, germination capacity and water uptake.

"It seems like the micro-malting approach gives you better footing from batch to batch, from year to year," he said. "We know exactly what we're dealing with and we'll develop a steeping cycle to suit that particular cereal, whether it be rye, barley or wheat, conventional or organic, and with the aim of achieving the optimum final saturation with the grain just chitting ex-steep.

"Each year it is slightly different than the year before, and of my 43 years I've being married for 38 of them. My wife has heard me say 38 times: 'I've never known a harvest like it.' This year is no exception, and so that's your annual curveball."

Garratt said they learn a lot from the first steep, and it's fairly consistent after that. "We can start off confidently that we're going to steep that grain for x hours at x temperature over a given period of days, and we can fairly accurately predict the outcome of having done that," he said.

"Rye and wheat are non-husk, and for that reason will demand less steeping, rye particularly. You have to actually aim for lower overall ex-steep moistures with rye than you would with wheat or barley. The carbohydrate softens very readily, and if you were to over-steep that, you would be in difficulty."

Admiral Malting steeping tanks, Alameda, CA

Steep tanks — often cylindrical conical-bottom tanks, but sometimes of a more traditional horizontal design — sometimes have aeration built in to provide oxygen to the grain as it respires and venting to pull out CO_2. Stephen Osborn of Stoutridge Vineyard and Distillery measures the production of CO_2 in the grain bed to help gauge progress in his steep.

"We dig a little hole in the top of a grain and put a CO_2 sensor in it so that we can monitor the CO_2 and we also monitor the CO_2 in the room," he said. "And by doing both of those, we can get a really good idea of biological activity and we can get an idea of [whether] we're in danger of suffocating the grain through CO_2 production."

He designed his double-tank steep system (described in Chapter 8) with overhead sprinklers and a recirculation system with six outlets underneath the grain bed. The recirculation system has a UV sterilizer to prevent biological growth and six air/water injectors. Steep water will recirculate from the middle of the tank to the bottom and top, with air bubbling through from the bottom.

"The aerobic condition discourages anaerobic bacteria, and I'm more concerned with anaerobic than with aerobic. Everyone talks about suffocating the grain, and I really built it under that theory," but he thinks that controlling bacterial growth is also a major factor in the quality of his malt.

After the initial steep, he'll pull the grain out for an air rest, giving it three rinses over the next 12 to 14 hours, both to help evacuate CO_2 buildup and to carry away bacteria. Once the second steep is complete, rather than cast the malt immediately, Osborn, a longtime winemaker and former biochemist, likes to let it sit.

"It may all be bacteriological, but we've found that post the second steep, if you let it drain for six hours, that can be helpful to getting an even start to the malt," he said. They'll pull it out of steep at 6 or 7 a.m., then dump it on the floor at noon or after lunch to allow CO_2 to collect and give the lactobacillus a good start at crowding out other growth. "That's really helpful for bacterial contamination. I know that by smell. I know very well the smell of malolactic bacteria, and lactic bacteria in general, and when we were first doing it I was going by smell."

While maltsters like Osborn and the Klanns at Mecca Grade Estate Malt have crops that can be watered with spent steeping water, most will see their steep water go down the drain, although some can be recycled. The water from the first two steeps tends to be more heavily soiled when it drains, but water from the third steep can potentially be reused for a first steep.

Outside of 100-year-old English malthouses with a concrete or stone tank, food-grade, 304 stainless steel is the material of choice for steep-tank design. Whether vertical or horizontal, a mesh or wedge wire false bottom helps to separate steep water from grain.

Chlorine filtration is important, and some method of attemperating the steep water — whether using a conditioned buffer tank, a heat-exchange system or blending warmer and cooler water — is necessary to maintain consistent steep temperatures. Crisp uses borehole water that generally stays at about 52°F year-round and steeps at about 60°F, Moody said, but the steeping patterns there still have seasonal variance because of changes to the ambient air temperature in the steeping room.

While there is a correlation between warmer water and faster uptake, he said there is limited value in increasing the temperature.

Hot water steeping "was a technique used to inhibit root growth, but it's not generally done. It was good for the yield, (for) efficiencies in the malting, but it wasn't good for the malt. You'd end up with a high yield of poor-quality malt."

Rick Wasmond, of Copper Fox Distillery, uses a wheelbarrel to move malt from the steeping tank to the floor.

Chapter Two

Flooring

Flooring in a modern malthouse is faster and more controlled than it used to be, yet very little has changed in 200 years. Steeped grain, ready to start germinating, is cast onto the floor where the maltster manipulates conditions to allow the grain to sprout and reach proper modification.

The addition of adequate moisture in steep prompts the grain to start its natural germination cycle. At the beginning of that cycle, the aleurone layer of the nascent malt kernel begins to create enzymes, including the amylases used by brewers and maltsters to break down starches and glucanases that degrade the beta-glucan matrix that makes up the cellular walls in the grain endosperm, where the starches are stored.

Freshly steeped barley is fragile, so a few maltsters dump the piece onto the malt floor and let it sit in larger mounds for a little while (depending on the season). In traditional English malting, the barley would initially be cast into two- to three-foot couches, or piles, which allows surface moisture to be taken in and some germination heat to start building. (Until 1880, malt in England was taxed based on its volume in couch.) When the malt began to chit — when the first nub of rootlet growth became evident on the kernel — it was then spread to 13–15 inches and finally out to a depth of three to four inches, at which point the green malt will cover 300–400 square feet per ton.

The process today varies from one malthouse to another, with some preferring to see the grain chit at the end of the final steep.

Many will cast the malt immediately to its final bed depth, which can also vary. Grain-bed depth is a crucial variable that the maltster controls. As the barley germinates, it releases heat. A deeper bed will retain more heat and create a higher temperature differential between the bottom of the bed and the ambient temperature. A grain-bed temperature of roughly 60°F is generally targeted.

Crisp couches the malt at 12 inches immediately after steep, helping any remaining surface moisture to be taken up by the grain and allowing a little heat to build to boost germination early on. It is then thinned out over the floor, thicker during the winter to retain heat and thinner during the summer to allow more heat to vent.

At Admiral Maltings, the barley is floored about four inches deep, which Ron Silberstein estimates is a little thicker than most maltsters would prefer. It's a result of his floor being slightly too small, but the glycol cooling in his floor helps him get away with it.

"We put it on the floor a little thicker, probably, than most," he said. "We have the malt turner and we have the radiant-cooled floor that's trying to keep the temperature down. It's probably about an inch thicker than optimal." At the moment he has two floors, about 5,200 square feet total, split between two halves, each designed to do 15,000 pounds. He wishes that he'd designed two halves at 3,500 square feet, instead of 2,600. A new floor that's in planning will hold more than ten tons and be about 4,200 square feet.

Commonly, maltsters will adjust their bed depth as germination progresses, maintaining a thicker bed early on to retain more heat and thinning the bed on day two or three as germination picks up speed and the grain gets warmer. Barn Owl's Devin Huffman has a roughly 1,700-square-foot floor that he uses for two one-ton pieces at a time. It's just a little less space than optimal, but he staggers his batches by two or three days, so that an older batch is taking up a little more floor space and a younger batch is set a little

Automatic malt turning machine at Warminster Malting, UK

thicker. Then the older batch gets thickened up as it finishes and the younger batch gets spread out as it starts to reach peak activity. As a result, the batches "sort of float back and forth across the center line" depending where they are in germination.

Joel Alex likes to keep the air temperature in the Blue Ox flooring space just below the target grain temperature. He poured a new slab in his space on top of the existing concrete, to be sure he was working with a fresh, clean surface. As a result, he has an eight-to-ten-inch thermal draw below the green malt. He generally floors for four days, but "the variety of the grain is definitely the biggest variable. You have to remember that we're working with a living organism," he said. "One of the opportunities with our scale is to work with alternative grains, including other types of barley."

He said that with nonstandard barley varieties or other unusual grains, which don't have as much data available, the key is to pay close attention to what the grain is doing. Alex will run trials and he's adjusted his schedule to help nonstandard barleys to properly modify. "We have had grain on our floor as long as eight days to bring it to spec," he said.

Air-conditioning and, in a few places like Admiral, cooled floors, are amenities that were not always available to maltsters. The air-conditioning at Crisp remains rudimentary, according to Moody, just enough that it "takes the edge off the temperature" when it's hot in the summer.

"Historically, all the floor maltings stopped production in the summer," he said. "You used to malt through about end of May or start of June, depending on the year and what the ambient temperatures were like. By then it was really a struggle to keep things under control, and then all the maintenance would be done" when the malting shut down for the summer.

The men who worked the malthouse would work on the farm through harvest, then come back to the malthouse to take in barley that would be malted from September through the winter and spring, when the ambient temperatures were more helpful.

With air-conditioning, maltsters are able to operate year-round. Moody said they might skip the initial couching during the summer, since ambient temperatures are high enough to help get the grain off to a strong, warm start. They still rely heavily on the traditional method of opening and closing windows based on the grain temperature, how cold it might get overnight and how much wind there is. It takes an experienced hand to keep from cooling the bed

Top— *Warminster workmen use a shovel to turn the malt.*
Bottom— *Raking the malt, a less aggressive method of turning*

too far and slowing germination or, conversely, not letting enough heat vent off, "and the malt would gallop away, and you'd spend the following day trying to cool it down," he said.

The maltster will also turn the bed periodically to help control the green malt temperature and to keep the growing rootlets from matting together. The traditional tools, still in use in many malthouses, are the grain shovel and the malt rake. Maltsters rake the bed from one end to the other to help turn the malt and break up rootlet mats or scoop up grain with the shovel and throw it to disperse the grain, homogenize it and strip heat. Some maltsters also use a rotovator, which mechanically turns over the grain bed.

Early in germination, the malt doesn't need to be turned as frequently, but it still helps in venting CO_2 from the bed and allowing fresh air to be brought in so that the grain can breathe. As germination progresses, more active care must be taken to keep the green malt from overheating. At Crisp, they'll initially make one turn with the mechanical turner per day, then another pass using the rake.

"The best method for doing that is to walk backwards pulling the rake with you," Moody said. "As well as dragging it down with you, you sort of pull it in a series of jerks so you end up with furrows down the floor, but if you look at it crossways you also get little peaks. It is turning it over and it's letting some heat out, but it's mostly about getting a big surface area on the malt to let more heat out of it."

Once the grain starts to heat up, it requires more raking to vent heat. When Moody worked for Guinness, they would turn the malt four times a day when germination was peaking: a rake early in the morning, again late in the morning, a pass with the turner in the afternoon and another rake in the evening.

While the English malting tradition discourages rootlet matting,

German texts that describe the *Tennen*, or threshing floor, indicate that some matting is preferred, with rootlet growth encouraged and matting allowed to proceed. A 24-hour period near the end of germination without any turning and reaching 70 to 71°F created "the gripping pile."[1] The CO_2 that would be trapped in the matted grain inhibited respiration as modification finished.

Sprinkling the grain with water while on the floor, once common in malthouses, is no longer considered an appropriate method. "It's a waste of time. At best you increase the root growth, you don't really get proper penetration of the water. It just tends to feed the embryo and increase the root growth a bit," Moody said. "You can't rely on increasing moisture content once germination has started, so you have to get the right amount of moisture into the grains in the steeping process. That's the key to the whole thing, really."

Most craft maltsters rely on one or two primary tests to verify proper modification and determine when to end germination: the smear test and the length of the acrospire, or the young plant shoot. The general target for acrospire length is between three-quarters and the full length of the grain, but this measure varies with barley variety.

The smear test is a more reliable approach if using multiple types of barley. The maltster squeezes a kernel of green malt between fingertips, and a well-modified kernel will smear to a paste of fine starch granules. An under-modified kernel will create a tacky gumball that indicates some beta-glucan has not been broken down. The smear test corresponds to the friability test done in the lab.

The same lot of grain will germinate differently over the course of the year. Barley has a natural cycle that corresponds with seasonal

---

1 Ludwig Narziss, *Die Technologie der Malzbereitung* (Ferdinand Enke Verlat Stuttgart, 1999), 226–227.

Sprouted barley ready for kilning

growth, so it can be more difficult to germinate freshly harvested barley than grain that has been sitting for a few months. At Crisp, Moody generally plans to malt the barley for a given harvest through October of the following year, and then begin the new crop in November, after it's sat for a couple of months.

"Our floors mostly malt winter barleys like Maris Otter. Harvest for this generally starts the second week of July," he said. "The barley generally performs better as it matures, as long as you store it in really good conditions. When you first start malting it in November, December, generally speaking it'll be a bit more sluggish and need time to warm up. As it gets into March and April, it will naturally want to start growing and it will require more turning and lower ambient temperatures to keep it under control."

The traditional kiln at Crisp Malting.
The malt here is in the early "free drying" stage.

Chapter Three

Kilning

If everything has gone right in selecting, steeping and flooring a batch of barley, the maltster has a batch of green malt that is properly modified and has a full enzyme package. It can be used for brewing and distilling, but it's not stable for storage. Kilning is the final key process; it reduces moisture to stabilize the malt, develops color and flavor and drives off undesirable volatile compounds.

Kilning for base malts, the vast majority of malting, consists of a few standard stages. Green malt comes off the floor still above 40% moisture, and most of the water needs to be driven off before the malt is heated to avoid denaturing the malt enzymes.

An initial withering stage of high airflow and low temperature will drive down the moisture level while keeping the malt below 120°F. High airflow is critical early on to prevent the malt from spoiling. Once the malt drops to about 15% moisture, it will hit the break point, where the free moisture has been driven off. At that point the bed enters the forced-drying stage, and the temperature needs to be ramped up to continue drying. During the withering stage, also known as free drying, air coming off of the grain bed is saturated with water vapor. After the break, the air coming off of the bed will be drier, and below 40% moisture it can be recirculated.

Finally, the curing phase brings the malt up as far as 185°F, depending on the style, bringing the moisture down to below five percent and creating any additional flavor and color in the malt. At Crisp, they get down to between three and four percent, Moody said. "If we're doing an ale malt, one where you want to push that flavor in there as well and you want to get some color into it, we'll go up to 180 or 185, just right at the end of the curing phase."

The very end of curing can determine the difference between similar types of malt, such as Barn Owl's lager malt and their pale malt, which differ by one degree Lovibond.

"They've got different character," Huffman said. "One a little more or less toasted and slightly more color, but the kilning process for those two products is very similar until that final finishing point, and that's when we would differentiate those two products."

Generally maltsters aim for a 24-hour turnaround on kilning, but producing different types of malt and different batch sizes requires some flexibility. "Our standard routine relies on us turning a batch of malt around every 24 hours, and if we can do it within fewer hours for the smaller batches, we then can buy some time for bigger batches," Warminster's Chris Garratt said.

For distillers malt, Crisp will let the grain sit in the kiln for two and a half days, starting with 125°F "until it's broken through, the last of the damp patches have gone off the top," Moody said, then ramp up as far as 140°F to preserve enzymes.

Huffman said that at Barn Owl they try to balance lower temperatures with the longer drying times they require. "Every time you lower the temperature by a few degrees, you add a couple of hours to the process," he said. "If we're trying to make a really pale product, we'll lower our pre-drying temperature, not dramatically, to try to keep from getting any pigment development or melanoidin development."

Kilning helps to improves the flavor of the final product by driving off the compound S-methylmethionine (SMM), which is a precursor to the off-flavor dimethyl sulfide (DMS). The presence of DMS results in a character often described as cooked corn or canned vegetable. In brewing, it has been associated with European lagers using high amounts of pilsner malt, because the malt is very gently kilned to prevent color formation and some SMM is left in the malt as a result.

At Admiral Maltings, the kiln floor is a fairly standard design of a wedge-wire false bottom, like a mash tun, with a plenum underneath creating positive air pressure that forces airflow through the grain bed. Crisp Malting's Ryburgh facility has a kiln that was first put into service in 1890 with coke/coal burners (which are still in place but no longer operational) and no forced air, relying on the Venturi effect for airflow through the chamber. "It's a slower process, but it really does bring out the best of the flavors of the malt," Moody said.

The most flexible kilns feature a fan with adjustable speed and the ability to recirculate air. "That's not a new trick," Garratt said. "Early maltsters were aware of that, not least its energy conservation. You don't have to keep conditioning cold air, but it can only be done post-break. Ultimately, toward the end of kilning, we can recirculate kiln air back to the fire for anything up to a hundred percent recirculation. So if you're making things like Munich malt or lactic malts, it's a very useful tool."

Devin Huffman said that it takes him "more energy to run pre-drying low-temperature air than it does to run our high-temperature finishing air because we're recycling so much of that heat that the energy demand goes way down."

The improved efficiency when drying base malts is not the only benefit of having recirculated air. It also expands the types of malts that can be made. Stewed malts, such as Vienna, Munich and caramel/crystal malts, are allowed to over-modify on the floor, and then will be kilned with high-moisture air recirculating. The

Top— The kilning room at Deer Creek Malthouse, Glen Mills, PA

Bottom—Workman loading coal into the kiln at Warminster Maltings, Britains oldest working malthouse

increased levels of starch exposed to heat and moisture promote the creation of sugars and amino acids. A roaster allows for further additions to a maltster's portfolio, with roasted malt being germinated, then roasted, while amber, chocolate and black malts are kilned, then roasted.

Large maltsters will often use multilevel kilns, with the drier piece at the bottom, on the finish deck, and the wetter, cooler piece on the floor above, on the withering deck. A piece will spend 24 hours on the withering deck and then 24 hours on the finishing deck. This is a more energy-efficient design with the same footprint as a single-level kiln, but also more capital- and time-intensive. None of the maltsters discussed in this guide uses such a system.

Most craft maltsters also use a static bed in the kiln, but a stirred bed, with mechanical agitators to mix the malt while kilning, allows a deeper grain bed in the kiln. Stirring will usually extend drying times, though, and the value of the square-footage gained has to be balanced against the expense of adding agitators to the kiln.

Maltsters have been battling with hazardous compounds that result from their drying fuel for more than 100 years. At the turn of the 20th century, arsenic-containing fuels, such as oven coke and anthracite, were used in direct-fire kilns. In the book Practical Floor Malting (1908), Hugh Lancaster warned of the creation of "arsenious oxide" in malt.[2] Barn Owl uses a multi-fuel kiln that relies partly on wood scraps, but they and other modern maltsters generally avoid direct-fire kilns because of the potential to create nitrosamines and polycyclic aromatic hydrocarbons (PAHs), both of which are carcinogenic.

---

2   Hugh Lancaster, *Practical Floor Malting* (White Mule Press, 2014), 91–92.

PAHs are particulate, so the airborne solids can be separated by proper design, and nitrogen compounds form only in high-temperature combustion. This leaves the door open for some modern maltsters, such as Copper Fox in Virginia, to expose their malt to low-temperature, smoldering fire to impart smoke character.

The most desirable flavor components — such as vanillin and the phenols guaiacol and eugenol — are water-soluble, so smoke must be applied either early in the kilning, or the grain can be finished in the kiln, moistened and put back in for smoking, as Alaskan Brewing Company and Colorado Malting Company do. "We're kilning the malt below five percent moisture... then smoking after the fact," Colorado Malting's Jason Cody said.[3] He believes it's easier for them to achieve the balance they're looking for by separating the processes into two distinct steps. They also use separate vessels for different types of smoke and bring the malt down to two percent moisture after smoking.

Geoff Larson, founder of Alaskan and author of the book *Smoked Beer*, uses "lots of wood chips" and recirculates the smoke for his alder-smoked malt, which goes into his signature smoked porter.[2] He noted that measuring phenol content, as is commonly done with commercial smoked malt, measures only one aspect of the smoke character. Bairds Malt measures their peat-smoked malt for ortho-, meta- and para-creosote.

---

3   Craft Maltsters Guild, Webinar: Smoking Malt, accessed Oct. 6, 2018, https://craftmalting.com/video/webinar-smoking-malts/

Maltsters use shovels to move the malt from the steeping tank to the floor at Leopold Bros.

Chapter Four

Grain Handling

While easy to overlook as a would-be maltster is focused on planning for steeping, germination and kilning, proper planning on how the grain is moved from one stage to the next can reduce the heavy lifting involved in floor malting and create an appropriately safe work environment.

Those "mundane" details caught Devin Huffman off guard when Barn Owl opened, but they can make the difference between a little work and a lot of work or the difference between smooth operations and bottlenecks.

"I spend much more time on product handling pre and post than I do turning grain on the floor," he said. "We were so focused on the malting that we overlooked the logistics and mechanics of grain transfers. We underestimated, for example, how many hours a week the seed cleaner is running in order to process the finished malt. We very quickly had to upgrade."

From raw material storage through to finished product, grain is moved repeatedly before finally going out the door, and a variety of options exist for handling that work. Raw barley is more durable than malted barley, so it can be handled with standard farm equipment such as a conventional auger. While grain silos are the most convenient storage option for large volumes of grain, many maltsters use super sacks or bins, depending on financial or space limitations. Augers are generally the preferred option to transport grain out of a silo, while augers or gravity-fed are both options for bringing malt into steep from a bin or sack.

At Blue Ox, Joel Alex prefers super sacks because of the flexibility they offer. Maine has a variety of farm types, from the industrial-agriculture size in the northern part of the state, where a small farm might be 300 to 500 acres, to southern Maine with more organic farms, where a large farm might be 20 acres. Bulk bags let him get malt from those smaller producers who can't provide a silo of malt. "You have this major difference in scale, and super sacks allow us to work with farmers at both scales," he said.

Coming out of steep, the barley has taken up a great deal of water and may have begun to chit. Pneumatic conveyors, belt conveyors, wheelbarrows and Boby barrows — classically used in English maltings and named for their original engineer, Robert Boby — are preferred methods of grain transport. Green malt also requires delicate handling when being moved into the kiln. Crisp Malting uses a power shovel to strip the grain off the floor and drop the green malt down a hatch, where it's transferred into the kiln via a spinning belt that pivots and throws the grain across the kiln floor.

Flex augers, which can run in both directions, and drag conveyors are sound options for grain or malt movement. Bucket elevators can be used for vertical moves to processes on another floor or in conjunction with gravity to drop grain into steep or through post-processing. When the vertical space is available, maltings will often gravity-feed kilned malt into a debearder/deculmer, which then drops the malt into a seed cleaner. The debearder will strip rootlets and acrospires from the kilned grain, then the seed cleaner will separate out the culms, broken kernels and undersized kernels. A variable-frequency drive is recommended on the debearder, which operates best when full.

Larger floor-malting operations tend to have their grain cleaned before delivery, ensuring greater homogeneity and reducing back-end losses; many smaller operations will work with their local farm-

Top— Super sacks of grain line the shelves at Admiral Maltings, Alameda CA.
Bottom— Common tools of the trade are a rake and a Boby barrow, at Crisp Malting.

Weighing bags of grain at the Copper Fox Distillery in Williamsburg, VA

ers to get a clean enough raw product and sort out the difference in post-processing. For those who are accepting less-than-pristine grain, a swim-out phase at the beginning of the first and possibly second steep may be helpful. During swim out, the steep tank is overfilled and the excess water, along with floating debris, dead kernels and other material, runs out of an overflow outlet. A gravity table is an effective way to clean up finished malt at a small malthouse. Stones and infected kernels flow across the top and bottom of the table, while the remaining good malt can be sorted by plumpness in the middle of the table.

Finished malt can be loaded into super sacks or bins for on-site usage, or bagged and palletized. A bagging/sewing line can range in complexity from a mechanical counterweight to an automated load-cell system, and bags should have, at the minimum, the kiln date included on them for tracking purposes. Pallet jacks and a forklift will be necessary to handle finished malt, if not earlier.

Pest management, including traps and an aggressive cleaning regimen, is a must-have in any malting operation. Some maltsters use diatomaceous earth to control pests, but DE must be handled with protective equipment to prevent inhalation and eye exposure.

Some of the greatest dangers in floor malting occur at the pre- and post-processing stages. Raw barley and kilned malt can both create significant amounts of grain dust, which is an explosive hazard even at very low levels. Dust should be collected in a cyclone system with a bag adapter, such as the Torit Cyclone, with collection points at each grain hopper and at the seed cleaner.

CO_2 venting is essential not just for the benefit of the malt or barley, but also for the health and safety of personnel. Auger equipment and vessels that personnel will enter to clean or service will also need to be equipped with lockout/tagout safeguards.

A forklift navigates the aisles between bags and super sacks of grain on the shelves at Admiral Maltings.

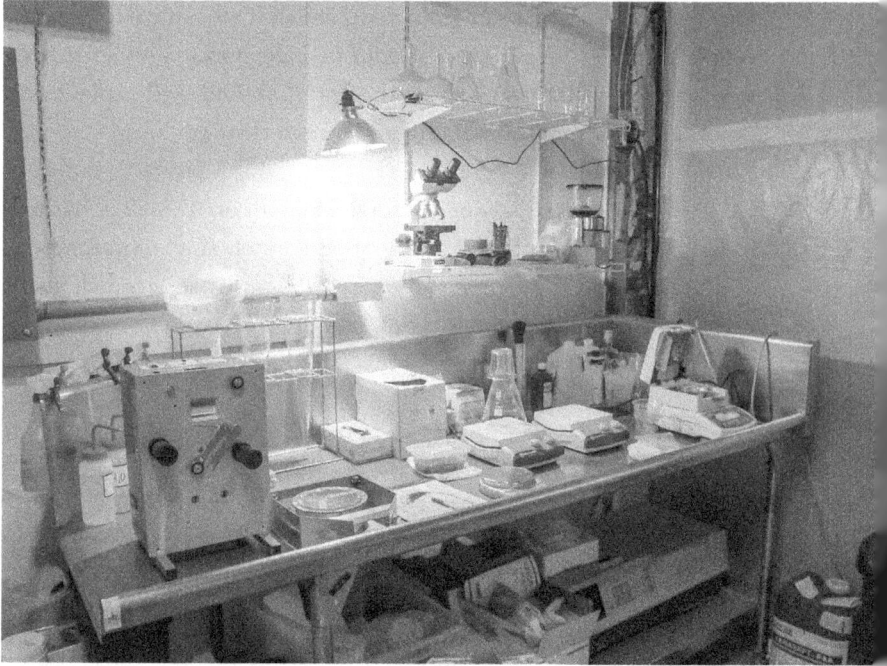

The lab at Deer Creek Malthouse

Chapter Five

Analytics

While malting itself isn't inherently difficult — it has been done for thousands of years to some degree or another — making consistent, quality malt requires a little more precision. Most craft maltsters operate with a modest lab operation, and there are some analytical tools that are crucial to doing the job well.

Thermometers almost don't even need a mention. Temperature measurement, whether manual, built into the side of a tank or a remote probe, should be ubiquitous. Possibly of equal importance is the moisture meter or moisture balance. A tool which measures the weight of the grain in its current state, then dries it down and measures the difference to provide a moisture level by percent, a moisture meter is the crux of a modern craft malthouse's process-data measurement. A small coffee grinder can also be helpful to break up the sample to allow for better drying.

As outlined in other chapters, moisture content is measured at steep, casting, daily during germination and through kilning. Along with temperature and time, it is a primary variable in malting and the importance of measuring it cannot be overstated.

Often, malt analysis is a hands-on process. Germination has historically been estimated by acrospire length and/or the smear test. Some maltsters believe that the length of the acrospire indicates modification, and aim for three-quarters the length of the kernel as an indicator of full modification. Others, such as Devin Huffman at Barn Owl, prefer the smear test, where the maltster squeezes a kernel of germinating barley to see how well it smears. A well-modified kernel will smear, while an under-modified kernel will be gummy.

"That's how we determine the end of flooring almost exclusively," Huffman said. "I find that the acrospire length is another indicator of modification, but it's not as reliable. It's really obvious when you're crushing or rubbing out germinating grain how well modified it is. For a somewhat objective measure, with a little practice it proves to be a very reliable method."

Chris Garratt of Warminster also feels that acrospire length is relative to variety and can be a false guide. "The old empirical tests, acrospire length and rub-out tests, we're doing all of that, but we don't make fixed decisions based on that," he said.

An old method used by Wendell Banks, of Michigan Malt, is to put a sample of the grain into a tea ball and boil for 30 seconds, then let steep for an additional 15 minutes. After the steep, the grain is cut lengthwise in half; starch that has been hydrated will look translucent and gelatinous, indicating modification, while starch that is not converted will remain white.

The germination test is commonly done in some malthouses, particularly with new grain streams (new crop year or farm) or with grain that has been sitting for months since the last test. Germination testing allows the maltster to adjust the steeping schedule for grains that take up water faster or slower.

The method outlined by the Craft Maltsters Guild involves 100-kernel samples of barley in four petri dishes, two each with 4 mL and 8 mL of water, incubating at room temperature. Over three days the germinated kernels are removed, and the germination capacity is the average of the 4-mL plates.

If the germination rate in the 8-mL plates is more than 20% lower than the rate in the 4-mL plates, then the grain may be water-sensitive and require more gentle steeping, such as four short steeps instead of three longer ones.[4] A friabilimeter tests modification of malt that has been kilned. The machine will break up and sieve out the modified grains or portions of grains, while the harder, under-modified part of the grain will resist breaking and be left behind.

For barley that performs poorly on the germination test, when the maltster needs to determine if the grain is dead or dormant, a germination capacity test can be performed by soaking the barley in a hydrogen peroxide solution. This will ensure the germination of any viable grains and help determine whether the grain is a loss.[5]

Some maltsters take additional steps in their on-site grain analysis. As a larger maltster, Crisp has farmers send samples of their grain to analyze for protein, germination capacity, screening and other general aspects, according to Moody.

Warminster also has a full lab at the maltings, Garratt said. "We couldn't imagine not being able to do that," he said. "We're very confident of what we do. We're only confident because we've already made malt with that grain, but you cannot 100 percent predict that you will hit that specification bang on."

Even if they're only doing the basics in-house, maltsters also need to be fluent in the factors that their customers — brewers and distillers, or themselves in either capacity — are looking for. This includes the information generally provided in a full-spectrum malt analysis. Virtually all of the American craft maltsters featured in this book rely on Hartwick College in Oneonta, NY, for their malt analysis, but other labs and public universities, including White

---

4   Craft Maltsters Guild, *Quality & Safety Manual* (Craft Maltsters Guild, 2017), 115.

5   *Quality & Safety Manual*, 117.

Labs, Michigan State University, the University of Vermont and Montana State University, also offer malt analysis services.

There are fairly tight requirements for barley to be good for malting versus feed. It needs to come in with moisture less than 13%, a high germination rate and protein between 9–13%. Protein is related to other factors. Higher protein reduces yield and creates haze; protein also corresponds with nitrogen, and yeast needs a certain amount of free-amino nitrogen for food. The Kolbach index indicates soluble protein versus total protein, which can have implications for free amino nitrogen (FAN), foam production, haze and color. While maltsters will generally look for a protein level below 12 to 13%, a few flavor-conscious distillers are happy to see higher levels of protein, at the cost of potential extract, with the idea that more protein means increased levels of flavor compounds.

Friability is an indicator of modification, as is the level of beta-glucan. Higher levels of glucans lead to trouble with mashing/lautering and filtration. Plumpness (6/64th screen) and extract are both indicators of potential yield, and color is indicated according to the Standard Reference Method (SRM) in the United States and the European Brewing Convention (EBC) method in Europe.

The enzymatic potential of malt is generally noted as diastatic power, which represents the total enzymatic package, both alpha- and beta-amylase. Some malt analyses may also note alpha-amylase separately. Depending on the end-use of the malt, testing for deoxynivalenol (DON), also known as vomitoxin, may be necessary. Produced by fusarium blight in grain, DON can survive the brewing process and carry over to the final product.

A fairly straightforward number that maltsters can look at is the yield of malt versus the starting weight of barley. With loss via growth (<5%), drop in moisture (from 13% in stored barley down to between 3–5% in finished malt) and rootlet and acrospire formation, maltsters will generally see around 18% of the starting weight lost.

Crisp works with about 280 farmers for their facility in Ryburgh, England, and they maintain a full lab for analyzing barley and malt. Moody said the farmers send samples to be analyzed for protein, germination capacity, screening and general characteristics, and they build a database of what they have to choose from. They select batches to go into the same silo based on nitrogen content and other aspects, primarily variety.

When the barley comes on-site, they check it again, more thoroughly, for physical attributes, nitrogen content, moisture and germination capacity, and screen it for small corns and other cereals or debris before putting it up for storage. They'll cut 100 grains in half and use a tetrazolium stain under vacuum, looking for 98% germination for every incoming batch, according to Moody. They'll also perform benchtop 4-mL and 8-mL germination tests to check if the barley is ready for malting. Samples will also be micro-malted in the lab to determine the best steeping and germination schedule, and then the malt is considered ready for commercial production.

In-process, Crisp tests for cast moisture or steep-out moisture. They may look at germination moistures in odd circumstances, but it's not usually necessary if the steeping is correct. "The process control on the floors is really the experience of the maltster, who is rubbing the grain and looking how far the root growth is, particularly the acrospire length," Moody said. "Getting that full modification is what you're looking for, and you can feel that in your fingers." Post-kiln, they'll run a standard full-malt analysis.

FINISHED MALT SPECS (Pale Malt)

Assortment: 80% plump, <3% thin
Moisture: 3–5%

Color: 1.5–3.5°L
Dry Basis Extract: 80%
Viscosity: 1.45–1.6 CPS
Kolbach Ratio: 35–50%
Free Amino Nitrogen: 130–200
Total Protein: 11–13%
Friability: 90%
Beta Glucan: <100 ppm
Alpha Amylase: >30° Lintner
Diastatic Power: 80–160° Lintner
DON: <1.0 ppm

The kiln at Leopold Bros. in Denver, CO

Chapter Six

Costs

Asking how much it costs to build and operate a floor malting is like asking how long is a piece of string. The answer is: It depends.

Much of the following information on a one-ton floor-malting system was provided by Adam Paul of Integrated Process Engineers & Constructors (IPEC) or culled from a presentation on a 1.5-ton setup that he gave to the 2018 Craft Maltsters Conference. It cannot be stressed enough that these numbers are purely hypothetical, and many are the result of assumptions that may or may not hold true for an individual in a given market trying to begin floor malting at a brewery, distillery or perhaps farm brewery or farm distillery.

A great deal depends on local utility rates, real estate costs, labor costs, taxes and other factors. These numbers should be looked at as a checklist to make sure everything has been considered, and are, as Paul said, "general order-of-magnitude values that need to be verified." Costs that need to be considered include education/training, utility rough-ins, lab/office space, grain storage, seed cleaning/debearding, bagging/packing, branding/marketing, equipment (capital and operational), real estate, utilities (capital and operational) and staffing.

A custom fabricator primarily with the pharmaceutical industry, IPEC got into the malting business by building the equipment for Blacklands Malt, in Leander, Texas, in 2013 and provides turnkey systems, which carry a commensurate cost. "Most people don't expect to see a half-million-dollar price tag on one of those AutoMalt systems," he said. "At the end of the day, you get what you pay for."

We have also sought to provide avenues where costs can be trimmed, either through manual operations or by applying the DIY spirit that imbues much of the craft-spirits and craft-beer industries, but we won't try to tell the reader the best way to engineer a kiln or what the absolute lowest-cost approach is. Trying to accommodate all of the variables involved would quadruple the length of this manual. However, we have tried to find alternatives where they are available.

"There are different ways to get to the finish line," Paul said. "The proof is in the pudding. If you run your system right and you have a good product and get high-quality, consistent results, who's to say what's right or wrong in terms of design?" He is a believer that floor malting provides the best-priced opportunity to get into malting. Box-malting systems carry a higher price tag and are more expensive to scale up.

An IPEC budget system costs approximately $55,000 for a manual one-ton steep and $240,000 for a manual one-ton kiln. That system includes digital timers for activities such as aeration and CO_2 venting, a 500,000-BTU natural gas furnace, adjustable speed for the blower and a proportional-integral-derivative (PID) temperature controller for the kiln. For another $15,000 on the steep and $30,000 on the kiln, IPEC includes an integrated programmable logic controller (PLC), touchscreen, recipe management system and remote access hardware.

Their AutoSteep System includes pneumatic valves, level sensors and temperature probes to work with the PLC to automatically follow a programmed recipe, while the AutoKiln includes automated temperature and blower-speed control and can be programmed to follow set schedules for free drying, forced drying and curing stages, as well as stewing. The PLC can also tie in to equipment such as a germination room chiller to integrate the entire process into the automation platform.

Paul said that, at $30,000 for the PLC and $45,000 for the full-automation package, the automation will often pay for itself. If the head maltster or owner can operate with one fewer staff member needed to "babysit" the malting process, then the additional equipment cost is quickly offset by reduced payroll costs.

For maltsters looking to trim costs and assemble their own system, dairy tanks have long been a source for craft brewers looking to retrofit and build their own equipment. Check the local scrapyard and industrial or agricultural auctions, and make friends with a welder, especially one who likes beer or whiskey. The build-it-yourself-er needs to properly size a steep tank to account for the fact that barley will swell by up to 40 percent in steep; more than 300 cubic feet may be necessary to fit a one-ton batch.

A few options are available for flooring materials. Many maltsters simply rely on a concrete floor that can be properly cleaned, so the floor itself may not add to the equipment costs. Some opt for food-grade tiling or an epoxy finish on their malting floor or will pour a new floor with glycol lines providing radiant cooling in the concrete. Costs for germination-room infrastructure and utilities will vary based on the facility (new versus retrofit), production rate (number of floors) and how the room is conditioned (radiant floor-cooling versus HVAC). Industry guidelines estimate that a maltster needs to vent 200,000 kilocalories per ton, requiring 235 kilowatt-hours plus five kilowatt-hours to overcome the ambient temperature outside the germination room. This equals 1.5 tons of chilling capacity per floor.

At Michigan Malt, Wendell Banks built his germination and kilning box for $18,000. The box itself cost $5,000, the wedgewire was $5,000 and fabrication – including two pressure places, a frame to support the false bottom, lid and running gear mounting – another $5,000. The remaining $3,000 consisted of the burner, running gear, air compressor and aeration stone.

The malting floor at Maine Craft Distilling.

Banks spent just over $1,000 for grain cleaning, weighing and milling equipment, but said $15,000 would be reasonable with a new mill and cleaner at $5,000 each. In total, he spent about $20,000 for a system that peaked at roughly 60 tons a year.

For turning the malt, a standard grain scoop will cost about $25 to $30. Maltsters will generally need to have a malt rake custom-fabricated, but that will be a less expensive way of turning than power tools, which can cost a few hundred dollars before customization. "It's a really excellent way to turn malt. It's more gentle on the malt," Joel Alex said.

Multiple options are available for kiln heating, depending on infrastructure and batch size. A gas furnace is the standard option, and can be sized for any operation and run on natural gas or propane. Gas furnaces are also relatively efficient, but can be expensive and difficult to operate with precision due to their large thermal mass and longer cool-down time. Sizing a furnace must be carefully done; kilning may not be an issue, but when "trim heating" an ambient space like the germination room, an oversized furnace operating at zero percent might still produce too much heat in the forced-air system. A budget-brand 500,000-BTU furnace can be found for under $10,000, though, as noted in the Kilning chapter, direct-fired gas heaters are not recommended.

Steam heating is an excellent option for the brewer or distiller already operating with a boiler and provides "a little more bang for your buck," Paul said. "Steam is an awesome way to heat a kiln. It's really efficient, very easy to control."

Steam systems can be sized for any malthouse, and one properly sized boiler can support multiple processes (brewhouse or distillery plus malthouse). Paul said $40,000 could be deducted from the cost of the kiln to use steam, though that savings has to be weighed against the cost of a boiler and steam/condensate field piping. For the brewer or distiller who already has extra boiler capacity or is purchasing a new boiler, "there should be a net savings," he said. Maintenance can also be simplified for the brewer/distiller, rather than having to maintain a boiler plus a furnace, and a steam heat exchanger will take up less space than a gas furnace.

On the other hand, a boiler might limit the maltster's options or require additional permitting. A boiler that produces less than 15 PSI is subject to less-stringent regulations, but will limit kilning temperatures to around 225°F, Paul said. This is enough to produce lighter base malts, but not darker kilned malts. To reach 300°F would require approximately 75 PSI steam, depending on the heat exchanger design, which falls under high-pressure permitting and regulations.

For a one-ton system, an electric heater can also be a viable option. "You might spend $25,000 for a furnace, or you can build an electric heater box and some controls, and it'll cost you five grand," Paul said. With proper controls, an electric system would have precision and responsiveness similar to a steam system and would be a smaller option than a gas furnace, though not as small as the additional steam equipment.

An electric kiln would be feasible only up to one or two tons, given the amperage required to heat process air at larger scales. It would require three-phase power and also likely be more expensive to operate, with higher kilowatt-hour-per-batch costs versus therms of gas per batch, though this will vary based on local utility rates. Paul recommends crunching the numbers to verify.

Those who want to roast malt will find that even small amounts will be costly. For a commercial drum roaster designed for 50 pounds of coffee, a maltster can expect to spend upwards of $20,000, increasing from there for larger volumes.

In addition to the heating aspect, any kiln will require a blower. Paul recommends a 7.5–10 horsepower blower for a one-ton kiln. He prefers the NY Blower brand, at $4,000 to $5,000, but a similar blower can be found at Grainger for $2,500 to $4,000. A variable-frequency drive should be installed with any blower system.

A kiln floor that will allow air flow-through is also a crucial aspect of designing a kiln. Structural stainless steel wedge wire is the industry standard, but will cost $200 to $250 per square foot, representing a significant portion of the kiln construction cost. Some maltsters use perforated sheets effectively, but Paul cautions that they must be supported adequately for the level of malt loading.

A wheelbarrow full of hydrated rye waits transportation from the steep tank to the malting floor, at the Copper Fox Distillery in Williamsburg, VA.

As described in the Lab chapter, most maltsters operate with a less-intensive analytical setup and rely on outside experts to provide complete malt specifications. Expanding on Paul's numbers, a few pieces of equipment are recommended for in-process management. A moisture balance will cost about $5,000, a friabilimeter around $7,000 and a spectrophotometer for optional rapid-color measurement will run about $5,500.

A good humidity sensor, which can run as high as $5,000 for models with a heated tip for saturated conditions, is helpful in monitoring off-air conditions that reflect grain moisture content, though many maltsters operate without one. A cheaper handheld meter can be useful for spot-chescking.

For a malthouse aiming to produce 150 tons/year, which would be 2.5 batches/week on a 1.5-ton floor malting, Paul estimates a maltster would need the following space: 1,500 square feet for grain storage, 550 square feet for grain cleaning, 300 square feet of office space, 150 square feet for a lab, 400 square feet for steeping, 1,500 square feet for germination and 600 square feet for the kiln, totaling 5,000 square feet.

A 50,000-lb silo, including the necessary concrete pad, can cost $12,000–$15,000, not including conveyance out. For producers located on a working farm, the United States Department of Agriculture Farm Service Agency may offer assistance in the form of grants or low-interest loans for equipment. There is great variability in the possible costs for moving barley and malt around. At the low end, malt can be transported for the cost of shovels and wheelbarrows or Boby barrows.

A used AT Ferrell Clipper 2B debearder will cost about $1,000, while Q-SAGE also produces popular debearding and seed-cleaning equipment. A bulk grain weigher/bagger will probably cost at least $5,000, and a cyclone for dust collection can be purchased for as little as $3,000, depending on size. Much of this equipment requires three-phase power in the malthouse. Would-be maltsters can also look for equipment supplied by industries that operate in similar ways. Blue Ox Malthouse, located in timber-rich Maine, had its kiln built by a local wood-kilning company.

INITIAL CAPITAL COSTS

Lot: $40,000
Building: $220,000
Utilities: $30,000
HVAC: $25,000
Ducting: $2,500
Malting Equipment: $315,000
Chiller: $20,000
Heat Recovery System: $15,000
Raw Material Storage/Handing: $7,000
Air Compressor: $5,000
Lab Equipment: $4,500

Tools: $1,000
Seed Cleaner: $9,000
Debearder: $7,000
Storage/Bagging: $20,000
Cleaning Equipment: $10,000
Equipment Freight: $10,000
Equipment Rigging/Install: $5,000
Startup/Commission Equipment: $15,000
Contingency: $75,000
Permitting: $1,500
Total: $838,000

ANNUAL OPERATING COSTS
Water (3 x 360-gallon steeps): $1,146
Water (germ): $91
Water (cleaning kiln): $200
Electricity - process cooling: $11,575
Electricity - equipment, motors: $13,785
Gas - process heating: $4,185
Gas - HVAC: $2,000
Insurance: $2,000
Taxes: $25,000
Employees (3): $105,000

UTILITY COSTS
for a 1.5-ton floor-malting facility (based in Madison, WI) used for estimates:
$5.30/1,000-gal H2O
$.60/therm natural gas
$.14/kWh electricity

Turning the grain at Admiral Maltings, Alameda, CA

Chapter Seven

Admiral Malting

Ron Silberstein just keeps going further down the rabbit hole.

Once an attorney practicing immigration law in San Francisco, he caught the leading edge of the craft-brewing wave, starting to homebrew in 1980, later taking the American Brewers Guild 10-week intensive course and interning at Marin Brewing Co. He went on to work at San Francisco Brewing Co. while assembling his own business, now called ThirstyBear Organic Brewery. In 2010, a farmer suggested that he could grow barley for the brewpub, but there was no place to malt it. That's when Silberstein turned his attention to malt.

Silberstein commissioned a farmer to grow a batch of barley and sent it to Colorado Malting Company to malt and ensure that it was going to be a quality product, later learning that Yolo County in the Sacramento Valley had been home to a thriving barley industry. Early 20th-century texts, such as Hugh Lancaster's *Practical Floor Malting* (1908), even extolled the virtues of "Californian" barley.

He was able to wrangle up the investors and put together a facility: Admiral Maltings turned out its first batch on August 25, 2013. Silberstein works with local farmers to contract malting-quality barley. Admiral has high standards for the grain it will accept, examining lots for protein content, plumpness, germination capacity, damage, skinned and broken kernels, pests, insects, disease and pre-harvest sprouting.

"All these kinds of things, we have to make sure it is OK," Silberstein said, "and if it is, then we pay a fairly premium price. And if they're not, the farmer will have to sell it as feed. Sometimes they nail it, and sometimes the quality of the barley isn't good enough for us to use."

As a maltster, he said that one of the critical aspects he looks at is the protein content. "We're not going to use barley that's 12 or 13 percent protein content because it doesn't make malt with enough extract for today's brewing needs," he said. But he wants to move users away from the commodity-malt mind-set, where flavor, freshness and aromatic qualities seem to have taken a back seat to extract and enzymatic power.

"Brewers tend to rely a lot on specialty malts for taste, or hops or yeast or barrel aging, but most haven't really focused on the essence of the malt — the flavor that comes from different barley varieties, the flavor that comes from different production techniques such as floor malting," Silberstein said. He specifically opted to go with floor malting over other options because brewers prefer floor malt, though he adds that it seems to be more of an academic reverence rather than actual use.

"We're not going to go out there and compete with Rahr," he said. "So we set out to do something that was distinctive and unique, and we're focusing on the quality of the barley, how it's grown. We grow no-till or organic."

The barley comes in from the mill where it's been cleaned and put into one-ton totes, and Admiral uses a bulk-bag unloader and a flex auger to bring it to the conical-bottom steep tanks to start the eight-day cycle. Once in steep, the grain will alternate between wet and dry cycles for 36 to 38 hours. An average schedule might start with an eight-hour wet cycle at 60°F, followed by 10 or 12 hours dry, then another eight wet and 10–12 dry and one more short wet cycle of a few hours. During the wet cycles Admiral aerates, and during the dry cycles, positive air pressure — a giant vacuum — evacuates CO_2 that the grain respires.

Once the steep is finished and the grain is at 44–46% moisture, they put a conveyor under the steep tanks and the grain gets loaded in Boby barrows, classic malthouse tools similar to a wheelbarrow with a central axle that allows one person to move and empty hundreds of pounds of grain at once. The grain is dispersed over a chilled floor built with PEX (cross-linked polyethylene) glycol lines running under the concrete floor to help control the temperature. They're aiming for 60°F, but there can be as much as a 10-degree variance between the cooled floor at 55°F and the ambient air at 65°F.

Because of the cooling in the floor, Silberstein can actually see the moisture level in the grain rise during flooring. "It draws moisture to the floor because the floor is colder than any part of the room. And so the grain actually absorbs more moisture while it's on the floor," he said.

They turn the bed two to three times a day using a custom-built turner, "basically like an electric rototiller," that has tines with high-density food-grade rubber scoops at the end. It aerates the malt, mixes it and disentangles the rootlets all at once. After four or five days, they hook a plow to a winch, inspired by what Crisp, Warminster and Scottish maltsters use, and pull the malt toward a central pit about 10 feet long and three feet wide, where the green malt is conveyed to the kiln. A fast-moving conveyor belt they call the "jet slinger," which Silberstein compares to a snowblower or a pitching machine, allows them to fill the kiln evenly without getting in and stepping on the malt.

He allocates 24 hours to kilning a batch, but it generally takes about 22 hours to bring the malt from about 45 to 46% moisture down to near or below four percent. He has a kiln that can produce base malts, such as pale or pilsner, as well as kilned caramel and darker Vienna or Munich malts. A 30,000-CFM fan runs heat over their four--million BTU indirect-fire heat exchanger and into the bottom of the kiln.

"That air can start at 120 degrees, but we can get it up to 300 degrees if we want to," he said. Once the kilning is finished, they push the malt to an auger inside the kiln that brings it to an elevator to the rootlet remover and a debearder, then into a seed cleaner to separate rootlets, chaff and broken kernels. From there it travels to a hopper for bulk sacks or 50-pound bags.

Admiral does a small amount of lab work, focusing primarily on moisture testing and tracking temperatures. They also do germination-capacity tests and have a friabilimeter, which indicates modification, but Silberstein relies on an outside lab for a full analysis.

As Silberstein looks at process improvements, he's planning to automate his steeping with their PLC. The new malt floor will require grain silos for storage. Looking back at lessons learned, adequate CO_2 venting was easy to overlook, and he underestimated the contact time necessary for the deculmer. Outside of equipment, he said, "I would have budgeted for a sales and marketing team from the start."

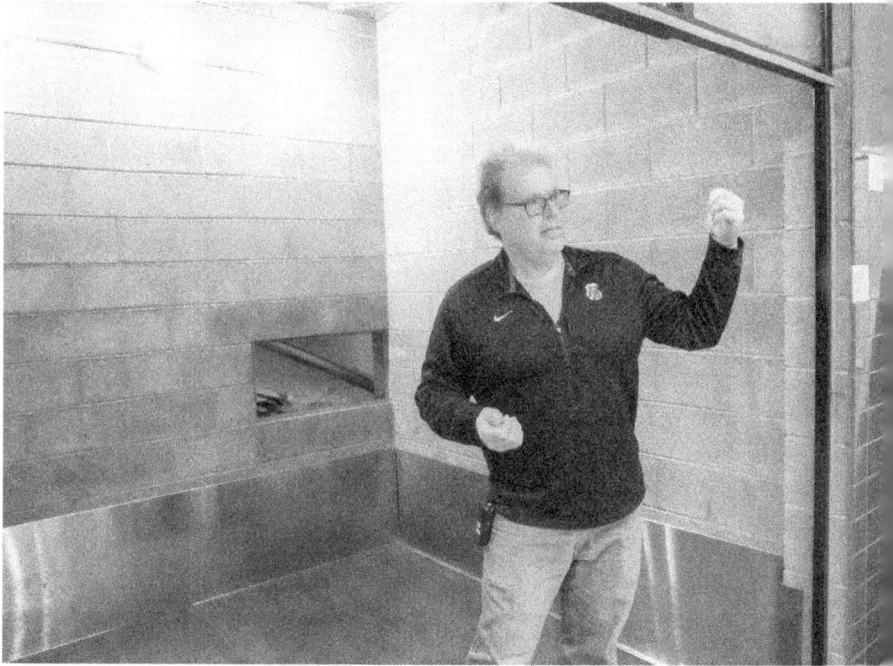

Steve Osborn at Stoutridge Vineyard and Distillery

Chapter Eight

Stoutridge Vineyard and Distillery

To retired biochemists Steve Osborn and Kim Wagner of Stoutridge Vineyard, malting their own grain was a no-brainer, on par with managing their own fermentations.

Osborn and Wagner bought the property, which goes back to 1902 as a winery and the mid-1800s as a farm, in 2001. They added a distillery to produce brandies and grape-based vodka, thinking it would be necessary for the business to succeed. After 10 years, Osborn said, the finances weren't an issue, and they decided to refit it as a whiskey distillery. Building a malthouse was naturally part of the program.

"We wouldn't have done a whiskey distillery without a malthouse," Osborn said. "We're into the flavor chemistry of natural processes. The fermentation and the malting are really the two places we have to shape it through biological action. There's no way I'm going to leave one to somebody else."

It's an outgrowth of the original mission of the winery: "to demonstrate the natural flavors in wine. And so if you're trying to demonstrate a natural flavor creation in whiskey, I'd like to be part of the malting."

Stoutridge is located about two hours north of New York City and uses grain from the surrounding Hudson Valley. In addition to brandies, gins and vodka produced from grapes, they produce a rye aged in barrels made from Hudson Valley oak, an Irish-style whiskey aged in a 1,300-gallon Barolo oval cask, a malt whiskey that's due out in 2025 and blends of eaux de vie and white whiskey aged in Pinot Noir barrels. Osborn uses his malt in both single malt and grain whiskeys.

"I'm always going for complexity of flavor. My distilling is very informed by my winemaking," he said. "I'm not trying to make any sort of traditional product, I'm just trying to sensitively build up a flavor profile that you might say when you taste it, 'Oh, maybe he's in New York, and maybe he's a winemaker.'"

Stoutridge runs two maltings a week, generally starting on Mondays and Thursdays, yielding about 2,000 pounds per week. Osborn designed the floor to fit four pieces, but has never run that much. He worries more about cleanliness than throughput.

One piece, at 1,000 pounds, comes out of a silo at four percent moisture. After hydration, it's about 1,300–1,400 pounds at 42–45% moisture, which gets kilned down to an unusually high eight percent moisture, coming in around or just over 1,000 pounds. The high moisture content hasn't been any trouble, since Osborn doesn't find himself storing malt for longer than a month. The system — both winery and distillery — is sized for a 600-gallon batch size with one half-ton malting per mash or cook.

Consistency hasn't been an issue, but Stoutridge works with Hartwick College for malt analysis, and Osborn uses a moisture meter to keep an eye on the malt as it's coming out of steep and during kilning, in particular. He has a 30' x 30' floor with a 20' x 30' space for hydration and steeping and a 10' x 10' kiln space off to one side of the germination floor.

Green barley comes in and is loaded into a storage bin, which then feeds the steeping setup, a double-tank system with a perforated

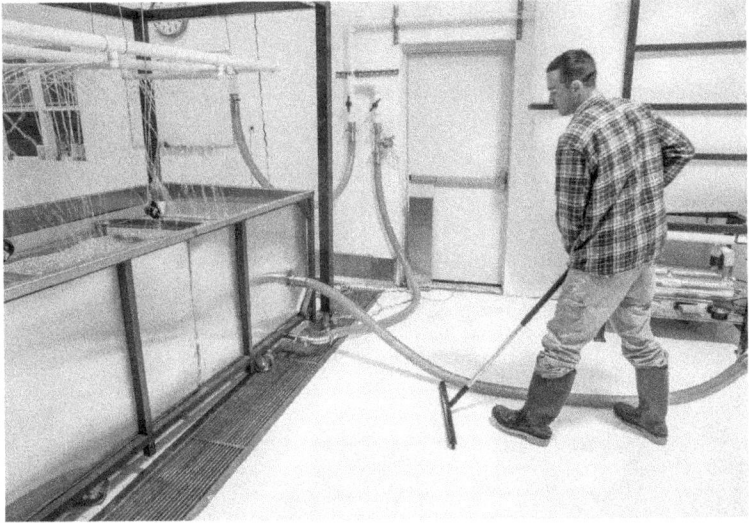

Top— A worker squeegees water into the floor drain next to the custom-built steep tank at Stoutridge Vineyard and Distillery.

Bottom— A couch of grain with a CO2 sensor inside begins to dry on the malting floor after being soaked at Stoutridge.

The heat source for the Angus MacDonald Memorial Kiln at Stoutridge

stainless dunking tank and an outer stainless bin about three feet wide, two and a half feet tall and eight feet long. Grain doesn't get deeper than about one foot in steep. The tank is on a frame with wheels and also has a winch on it so that it can be rolled or moved, preventing hidden areas that can't be cleaned.

Once in steep, the barley receives an initial rinse to remove dust, and then soaks for eight to nine hours, recirculating with aeration and UV sterilization. Stoutridge will air-rest it for 12–14 hours and dunk it again for an eight- or nine-hour overnight steep before casting at between 42–45% moisture. Located on a limestone aquifer, Stoutridge gets 60°F well water, and spent water from the steepings is reclaimed for the vineyard.

Once the malt is ready for germination, they'll pull the perforated bin out and carefully lift one side, tipping it upside down and leaving the malt in a mound for the first hour. After that, they'll rake it a little, just to even off the top, then rake it to one-foot thick after another hour. In another two to three hours, they'll take it down farther.

"I'm worried about the very first little rootlets, you have to be very careful with those," Osborn said. "When the rootlets get a little bigger, they're actually more durable than you'd believe, but when they first start, the whole thing is kind of fragile."

He'll set the grain depth to about six inches for germination, varying it depending on whether it's too wet or dry, too warm or cold. They're closely monitoring temperature, though at the beginning of germination it takes longer for the grain temperature to change. Osborn designed the building with radiant floor-temperature control as well as ambient air-conditioning, "so we can get the malt from both sides." The moisture content coming off the floor is still about 42%. Osborn had been worried that running the air conditioner would dehumidify the air too much and pull moisture from the grain, but that hasn't been an issue.

They turn the grain every 12 hours, generally giving every batch seven or eight turns, or about four days on the floor, and stop when the acrospire is half to three-quarters the length of the grain. For the first few months, Osborn said, they would turn the malt every four hours. That meant someone had to get up at midnight to rake it, and someone had to be in at 4 a.m. to turn it again. When Aaron MacLeod from Hartwick College came to visit, "He just looked at me like, 'Are you joking? You don't have to do that.' We didn't notice any difference in the quality parameters of the malt by doing less turning. We just had to work a lot less."

Once the green malt is fully germinated, it gets shoveled into the kiln enclosure, which is essentially a slotted floor inside the widened-out chimney of the furnace, located directly downstairs.

Inside the kiln, the depth of the green malt is about 18 inches, dropping a couple of inches by the time it finishes.

Channels from the roof draft air back down into the big native-stone kiln, which is primarily run off of a 25-kilowatt electric heater. The heater is powered by 300 solar panels and uses excess heat from the floor-cooling system, as well as a little bit of propane. "The solar gets it up to about 100 [degrees], and then the furnace gets it up to about 110, 120."

Osborn prefers a light touch in the kiln, going in at 110–120°F for two to two and a half days. Because he's doing open-top fermentation in fir-wood fermenters — trying to cultivate the distillery's microbiome into the whiskey profile — and using a direct-fire still, he's aiming to develop flavor and subtlety through those processes rather than creating heat-related flavors in the malting process.

"I may be different than a lot of guys in that I don't really go above about 130°F," he said. "I don't want to cook my proteins. I'm not trying to get Maillard [reactions]. My pot still is a direct-fire still, and so I'm trying to sort out flavors developed through pyrolytic reactions in the heat of the still and see if I can feature that instead of Maillard [flavors] in the malt. I really want my malt to taste just like grain, like malted grain. I don't want it to taste toasted."

After kilning is finished, the grain is shoveled out to a conveyor, which fills a 2,000-pound super sack. The bagged grain moves via trolley winch and is fed into the deculmer, then the seed cleaner. "One way you know your moisture content is correct is when that all works right, because if the moisture out of the kiln is 10 percent or more, it just turns into a real nightmare trying to clean it," Osborn said. "It doesn't take much out of spec for the equipment to object to what you put into it."

They load the finished malt onto another winch and send it down to the mill. Once it's milled, they winch it over to the mash/lauter tun to brew with. "I can deculm, clean the grain, mill it, get it in the bag, get it prepped to go into the mash tun, get the area completely cleaned and swept in an eight-hour period with a lunch break," he said. "So I'm happy with that. I could do one of those in a day and keep the area clean so we're not getting too many mice around."

Rick Wasmund talks on the phone as he walks past fruitwood used to smoke grain at the Copper Fox Distillery, formerly the Lord Paget Hotel, in Williamsburg, VA.

Chapter Nine

Copper Fox Distillery

Inspired by the rich, handcrafted flavors of Scotch and the idea of making a single malt whiskey smoked with what's available in Virginia, Rick Wasmund took an idea and transformed it into a distinctly American brand and two distilleries.

As one of the first American malting distillers, he started with a concept in 2000, followed by an internship at Scotland's Bowmore distillery — one of a handful of Scotch producers that still floor-malt their own grain — and opened the first Copper Fox Distillery in Sperryville, VA, in 2005.

"The idea began with the idea of making a single malt whiskey with malts that were smoked differently," he said. "Applewood, cherrywood was indigenous, local stuff that I use in cooking and that I thought would be good in whiskey. When I looked for whiskey to buy that was made that way, there wasn't any."

From the beginning, Wasmund was dedicated to malting all of his own barley and rye. In 2015, he bought a property in Williamsburg, VA, to open up a second distillery and expand malt production, and now sells excess malt to local breweries and distilleries.

Both locations offer the ability to imbue his malt with unique smoke character. Wasmund's namesake single malt is produced with both applewood and cherrywood smoked malt, but he also offers a peachwood single malt, a peachwood bourbon and a rye blended with apple- and cherry-smoked malts. His grain comes

Grain from a steep tank sits in a wheelbarrow ready to be spread onto the malting floor, at the Copper Fox Distillery in Williamsburg, VA.

from a couple of different Virginia farmers in primarily the northern part of the state, a good growing region where barley is sown in the fall, spends winter in the field and wakes up again in the spring to be harvested in May or June.

His Sperryville Copper Fox facility was modeled after the Bowmore distillery. He started out with a smaller steep tank; it was on wheels and they could dump grain straight out of it onto the floor in a serpentine pattern and then even it out. Now, with a bigger steep that's fixed in place, they pull the grain out into wheelbarrows and dump it onto the floor.

Steeping schedules at Copper Fox vary with grain variety, time of year and how long the grain has been sitting, even from one malthouse to the next, depending on water and weather conditions. The water in Williamsburg is a little warmer than the well that Sperryville employs, so Wasmund has to adjust for that.

"We might soak for eight hours in Williamsburg, and then 14 hours [air] rest and then a 10-hour hour soak. Then maybe a quick one-hour soak for the third day after another 12 hours' rest," he said. "None of that is static and that requires some science, knowledge, art, whatever you want to call it, but you've got to make adjustments along the way."

The grain spends five days on the floor, depending on the temperature he's able to maintain. From the floor, the grain is loaded into a tipping bucket and picked up with a forklift to the raised kiln to dump and spread out. "The kiln in Sperryville is big enough to walk under, and we have a wood stove under there, the fans, perforated steel floor, and that is very conducive to smoking," Wasmund said.

In Williamsburg, he built in additional capacity, some of which is going to other users. The system there is designed for 6,000 pounds twice a week, but they generally run 4,000-pound

Top— Grain dries in the kiln at the Copper Fox Distillery, Sperryville, VA.

Bottom— A malting rake sits amid green rye that is germinating on the malting floor at the Copper Fox Distillery in Williamsburg, VA.

batches. The floor in Sperryville is cement-coated with a food-grade epoxy to improve cleaning and mold control, but his solution in Williamsburg was to use porcelain floor tiles with mold-free grout, which is "quite a bit easier to keep clean."

The kiln in Williamsburg is located below the malt floors, so when it's time to transfer green malt into the kiln, they shovel it down a couple of hatches that chute the grain into the kiln, where it needs to be spread out. They're no longer able to get underneath the kiln, but instead use forced air to dry the malt.

While the new malthouse has the capacity to put smoldering wood in-line to smoke the grain, Wasmund said the new location is mostly unsmoked malt going out to other local users. "Not everyone is as fond of the smoke as we are," he said. Because the drying in Sperryville is a little uneven, he added, they get a little bit of roasted grain at the bottom of the bed.

"I think we'll probably rebuild the kiln in Sperryville, having an efficient fan that works, saving the heat and being able to recirculate the air to get the temperature up and then blasting the humidity out," he said. "A lot of the heating depends on the relative humidity externally. And then, if you're not concerned about the conversion aspects, you get into some flavor aspects of roasting the grain, but that requires quite a bit more heat, especially if you want a dark malt."

They use Hartwick College for a full-spectrum analysis. He doesn't worry about the malt they use in-house, but has an analysis done for the malt that goes out to customers. For his own malt, Wasmund relies primarily on a moisture meter to keep an eye on things.

Chapter Ten

Barn Owl Malt

At Barn Owl Malt, where Devin and Leslie Huffman floor-malt local barley in Ontario, pigs are feeding on culms and a rooster is crowing. It's the old family farm, his grandfather's place.

"It was a working farm in the late '80s," according to Devin. "We've got a bit of a funny farm here, nothing too serious." Rather than trying to buy their way into cash-cropping when they took the property over, he said, they decided to look for a more value-added niche market, yet something that was tied in to agriculture. They started looking at farm brewery ideas, then they looked at the supply chain and "found this big hole" where there was no local malt. Hops have been growing in the province for 10 years, and there's a history of barley being grown there, though it's a challenging climate for both crops.

"We were even finding a lot of grain growers that were approaching the brewers directly and not necessarily having a full understanding of the supply chain," he said. They decided to step in and bridge that gap between grain growers and the quickly multiplying craft brewers.

Opened in 2016 after two years of development and construction, Barn Owl sources barley from farmers around the province of Ontario, which has a diverse array of weather patterns and microclimates. If there's a major failure in one area, they can lean more heavily on another. A big feature of Barn Owl's approach is that their malt is entirely single-stream; all of the grain in a given batch will come from a single farm and can be traced by the brewer or distiller all the way back.

"We work with some farmers that are tenth-generation landowners and have a long and interesting history of farming in the province," Huffman said. "By keeping those grain streams unblended, we can offer breweries in different regions of the province grains that are from their region or as close to it as possible."

It increases the brewer's interest in promoting the farm it was grown on and the history of the region and boosts the regional identity in the Ontario craft scene. It also gives Barn Owl the ability to malt each grain stream separately, paying attention to how to treat it best rather than trying to find an average of a blend of barleys.

The Huffmans decided to floor-malt instead of buying a pneumatic system for a few reasons, including price and availability. Since they had to put up a building either way, the equipment outlay was simpler and less expensive. There were few options for turnkey systems at the time, and they were very capital-intensive relative to the malting capacity. It also gave them the chance to be more creative with their malting.

In the years since, the availability of turnkey, all-in-one box maltings has increased, but now that they've gotten a taste for floor malting, there's no going back. "The more we got into it, the more we looked at the history of floor malting. And then once we started actually operating and seeing the character of the product that we were able to bring out with floor malting, we became more and more enamored with it," Devin said. "It gives us differentiation. It offers us something that is distinct in the market — in the story, in the heritage, but also in the character of the product."

Floor malting allowed them to build in extra production capacity as well, giving them room to grow without having to reinvest in equipment right away. Having steeping, flooring and kilning all in separate spaces gives them the ability to adjust production levels with more flexibility than a box system, using the same vessel for multiple tasks, would. Barn Owl can stagger batches as close as two days, meaning they can start and finish a batch every 48 hours. That would require much more investment if they were operating with box-malting systems. They designed the facility for a batch size between 2,200 and 2,750 pounds, and the system is scaled so they can move up to batches of more than two tons by installing a second floor.

Huffman likes to run his malting low and slow, keeping the germination room at 57°F with steeping water coming in at 52 to 53°F in the winter, "right on the edge" of being warm enough to prompt the barley to sprout. "We have the capacity to adjust the temperature, but we've had really good results with modifying our process around the seasonal variations," he said.

He plans for roughly two days to fully hydrate the grain, depending on lab trials, with a standard mix of immersion periods and air rests. He knows that once they establish the water-uptake behavior of a particular grain lot, by keeping the grain streams independent they're able to hydrate the grain evenly, consistently and precisely.

The malt will germinate for four and a half to five days, and Huffman will try to keep the temperature low on the floor. It "gives us a lot of flexibility, gives us some forgiveness," he said. The floor depth will average about four inches, thicker on the first couple of days and thinner when the heat production ramps up on day three or four. He uses a combination of raking and shoveling, depending on how busy they are and what stage the grain is in. There's a trade-off: Raking is easier but doesn't strip as much heat, while "the shovel is high-intensity, low-frequency, so we can get away with fewer turns or less frequent turning."

Huffman might give it a shovel-turn first thing in the morning if he knows he's going to be out making deliveries most of the day, whereas, if he'll be around all day, he might rake it once in the morning and as needed at midday. He'll turn the grain at least twice and up to three times per 24-hour period. "For the first 48 hours after being cast on the floor, we've got a bit of forgiveness, we don't have to turn it as regularly. By day three and four, we've got to be watching it pretty close."

The Huffmans designed and built their own kiln, so it's not an off-the-shelf model, but the concept is straightforward and based on standard industry equipment specs for fan size, air volume and temperature capabilities. "We were looking at kilning parameters based on certain types of malts that we intended to produce," he said. "Essentially, we designed our kiln performance around the parameters to be able to produce those malts specifically."

They're using a shallow-bed kiln, with a grain-bed depth of 20 inches or less at the beginning of drying and dropping to four or five inches by the end. It lets them get away with a static bed during kilning. Because they don't have natural gas, they designed a multi-fuel kiln, using wood by-product from a local manufacturer and a three-stage heating system. "The use of a local by-product as fuel has saved significantly on our operating costs," Huffman said. Since kilning is the most energy-intensive stage in malting, "efficiencies in kiln-heating systems can pay for themselves very quickly," he added.

They have limited lab equipment, with a moisture balance service as the workhorse for day-to-day analytics. They monitor the moisture content closely during steeping, though sampling during germination is more of a long-term monitoring approach. "If there's any concern over some change in the relative humidities and weather patterns, we might keep an eye on it just to make sure that the moisture content's not dropping too rapidly during the germination period," he said. They keep a closer eye on kilning because the batch sizes at Barn Owl vary. He loads the steep tank by volume rather than weight, so one piece may come in at 1,800 pounds while the next could come in at 2,400 pounds, which changes the drying profile slightly, resulting in different times for each temperature stage.

Being located on an agricultural property means that Barn Owl is able to use conventional agricultural grain bins for barley storage, "which is extremely cheap compared to storing everything in totes in a warehouse," Huffman said. Finished malt is bagged and stored more carefully to control moisture and humidity, but they don't find themselves keeping much malt in inventory.

Unmalted grain, which is more durable, is moved around with conventional grain trucks and augers. An auger is used coming straight off the kiln to help improve deculming. With dust and friability more of an issue with finished malt, Huffman relies on bucket elevators and gravity and is planning to transition some of his augers to a pneumatic system for post-cleaner handling, which will offer greater flexibility. "The fact that we use multiple grain streams that aren't being blended means we end up having a larger number of storage containers. We have to have a storage container for each of the grain streams, and the logistics of loading the malthouse with grain becomes a little bit busy, and conventional augers can be a little bit limiting because you can only go in one direction."

The malt is transferred out of steep into a wheelbarrow, where it gets spread on the floor, then it's wheelbarrowed again to load the kiln. Once it's dry, they'll use conveyors to transfer it. A pneumatic conveyor goes to the deculmer, then a bucket elevator feeds the cleaner.

Another part of materials handling that was easily overlooked is the health and safety aspect and the accompanying regulatory implications. Opening the first floor malting in Ontario led to plenty of headaches, as government agents tried to understand what they were looking at and how to classify it. Unlike with breweries, which handle a great deal of malt and have many overlapping health and safety concerns with explosible grain dust, there was no set precedent, no other examples in operation to look at.

"There was no business-as-usual allowance for that sort of thing, so we were scrutinized very closely and offered very little forgiveness, to the point that we were constantly being pushed into a higher bracket of risk than what we probably were," Huffman said. "There was nothing in the building code or even in municipal bylaws or provincial bylaws specifically outlining requirements for a malthouse. At one point they wanted us to comply with the grain elevator regulation, which is extremely prohibitive in terms of types of wiring and electrical systems, special motors and even switch covers, not to mention the insurance complications. So the grain handling is easy to overlook, but can be very problematic."

Pre- and post-process handling were the biggest concerns. Transferring grain from trucks to silos and from silos to steep tanks, along with post-kiln processing such as deculming, cleaning and bagging, are where the major dust-related hazards exist. Once the grain is wet, dust issues are eliminated. Working with augers and grain bins also creates pinch points and safety concerns with respect to grain being loaded and unloaded.

"That's part of the reason our planning and construction took two years, because there were some points where we were stalled for four or six months dealing with the electrical safety authority or local fire regulations," he said. "There was nobody else operating at this scale in the province. There was no facility to look to in terms of solutions, so any operating parameters that we gave to the regulating bodies were all on faith that we were actually going to build and operate as we were describing."

Huffman's local farmers are primarily growing AC Newdale, followed by AC Metcalfe, and Barn Owl maintains supplies of both. Huffman said Newdale has been a particularly good malt for the craft market. "It's a highly aromatic, flavor-forward malt. When we're finishing a product and we want to throw the flavor profiles one way or another, the Newdale seems to respond very well to that. Using the same barley, we can produce several different products that are really nicely distinct from each other. The lighter malt styles have floral characters, some white flower flavor and aroma, and then we can also drive up to more nutty dried-fruit profiles."

Newdale has a slightly lower enzyme profile, and when finished as a robust pale ale malt can make for a nice substitute for more "charismatic" European malts such as Maris Otter. Metcalfe is easier to grow, with a higher enzyme content and more subdued flavor profiles, making it good for use as an adjunct barley or when the malt flavor is not the focus.

In addition to barley, Barn Owl malts wheat and rye. Those "naked" or huskless grains take up water differently than barley, requiring discrete management but no additional equipment. Rye is particularly sticky and fragile during germination; Huffman said it's prone to crushing and smearing.

"When you're walking through to rake it or shovel it, your boots get all packed up with it like clay, so it's a bit harder to handle," he said. "It shrinks a little bit differently in the kiln than barley does. It tends to pull away from the sides instead of just shrinking down, so you need to keep an eye on it because you can end up with short circuits where you're not getting air moving through the grain bed. It's just blowing right past."

Barn Owl deals with multiple waste streams from their malting operation. The seed cleaner has different outputs for undersized kernels (small grains and broken kernels) and another for dust and chaff. They tried working with a local dairy operation, but ran into too much variation in the final product for the strict feeding regimens of that industry. Instead, they give it away to a few local farmers for beef cattle, and they raise some pigs themselves.

The culms are a bit harder to move, Huffman said, because animals won't eat them unadulterated. "We have some local farmers that take it and blend it with corn and molasses, and then the cows will eat it," he said. "We have several small farms, hobby farms, taking the product.

"We didn't want to get into selling our by-products, because we'd be more heavily regulated selling animal feed than we are selling malt for brewers. We would have to redesign the whole process to accommodate it, then we'd have to have batch testing to have nutritional information."

They're looking at pelletizing the waste material, either for feed or to help fuel the kiln. Huffman said he could reduce the waste produced by having their seed pre-cleaned, but that would add to the final cost of the product and add logistical issues of transporting it to and from a cleaning plant. Small, independent seed-cleaning plants are becoming increasingly rare as well, meaning he'd have to ship the grain "all over the province" to get it done. Huffman has found a middle ground where he works closely with farmers on their agronomic practices, "right down to the settings on their combines," to help him get a consistent enough and clean enough product, taking a few extra percentage points of loss over the additional cost and processing.

Top— Dr. Edwin Sloper Beaven bred the Plumage Archer strain of barley that is the ancestor of today's Maris Otter.

Chapter Eleven

Warminster Maltings

Not much has changed over the years at the malthouse in Warminster. The faces are different, Guinness has come and gone, but the operation now known as Warminster Maltings pushes on much as it did 20 years, 50 years, even 150 years ago.

Malting at Warminster, once the biggest market town in the English southwest, began as early as the 1855 harvest by William Morgan and was handed down to his son, William Frank Morgan, whose name is still etched above one of the entryways. The younger Morgan later passed the maltings on to his brother-in-law, Edwin Sloper Beaven, who bred the Plumage Archer strain of barley that remained prominent through much of the 20th century and was a forerunner of Maris Otter. Beaven's interest in barley research and breeding led to work with the young Guinness Research Laboratory, laying the foundation for further association between Guinness and the Beaven family.

The maltings survived a fire in 1924, and, after Beaven's passing, his daughter Alice managed the business until Guinness took full ownership of the operation, but not the building, in 1947. In May of 1994, Guinness announced that the maltings would be closed, along with other malthouses in Norfolk, East Anglia. Chris Garratt, who had worked for the company since finishing school in 1975, organized the new Warminster Maltings, Ltd. to carry on work at the facility.

In 2001, Robin Appel, one of two individuals with exclusive rights to the Maris Otter strain, bought Warminster and hitched it to the burgeoning craft-beer scene and his access to Maris Otter malt, to great success. In 2010, Appel recounted the history of the maltings in Warminster in greater depth in the book *The Malt-Stars of Warminster*.

"The basic steeping and germination has changed very little since the maltings was built in 1855," Garratt said. "We've got the separate steep, we've got independent germination floors, we have the ability to steep whatever length we need. So we've got no limitation on the flexibility of steeping or germination periods."

Hand throwing malt at Warminster to turn, aerate and cool it.

Garratt said that part of the reason he was able to salvage the Warminster operation while the other two facilities closed was because the Beaven family had retained ownership of the building. As the head maltster of a storied facility, Garratt is one of six men to have helmed the operation at Warminster during its many years. "We benefit from having that rich heritage. It gives us pedigree and provenance," he said.

The Warminster facility contains four steep tanks and four pairs of floors that can handle four batches each. Garratt can take in batches as small as 5 tons, but generally does larger batches. "We are very pleased to be able to do very special runs of individual bits and bobs. That is something we cherish being able to do," he said.

His steep tanks are flat-bottomed, with no aeration, spraying or CO_2 removal, "and we're quite comfortable with that," Garrat said. They use well water, which can be attemperated to a target range of 52–59°F if it comes in too warm or too cool. Garratt's steeping temperature range is on the low end, but he believes this gives better reproducibility between batches. "We're not looking to speed up the production. So we are tending to always hold back the barleys rather than looking to push them," he said.

Steeping times for each wet could be anywhere from six hours to 15 hours, with two to three wet cycles and alternating air rests and a target of about 45% moisture. "The higher the moisture, the more active it's going to be on germination. So if you if you want to hold things back a little, you can just reduce the saturation level," Garratt said. "As a good rule of thumb, don't get too overambitious on moisture levels above 45 [percent], that's about as high as you'd want to get."

Flooring, aside from the addition of some power tools, has perhaps changed the least of all at Warminster. (A careful eye can even see where, in the 1800s, the malt was couched before being leveled onto the germination floor.)

While they take full advantage of the ability to have air-conditioning, which results in bigger batches and the ability to malt year-round, airflow is controlled for much of the year in the traditional way: opening and closing windows. The maltings are laid out in two buildings, with a courtyard in between that narrows slightly at one end. As a result, the Venturi effect creates a draft through the courtyard.

"Whenever you stand in that courtyard, summer or winter, you'll feel a breeze, which enables us to open or close the windows and have circulation" on the malt floors, Garratt said. "Prevailing winds and sun direction and all those things are very important to us."

Malt is on the floor four to four and a half days in the summer and up to five days in the winter. It gets turned three to four times a day, with a combination of a Robinson turner, which resembles a rototiller, and a Redler power shovel, which is a horizontal plow pulled by a winch. They use the Redler to level the malt during germination and to pull the green malt down the floor into a trough conveyor to go to the kiln.

In the kiln, the malt is leveled manually, with care taken not to trample it down and compact the bed. Of Warminster's four kilns, which have been converted to gas-fired, Garratt said number two is the most modern, refurbished in 1950 with forced air. The other three have fan-assisted airflow, but primarily use natural ventilation.

Once kilning is complete, the finished malt is shoveled out into ducts in the bottom of the kiln floor, into a hopper, through a deculming screw and then into a sieve. The malt is analyzed by a full-time lab technician, and within the day they'll make a decision on where to put that batch of malt and whether it gets blended with a similar batch.

"We've got several hundred tons of storage on-site, so we've got enough of what we need for immediate sales," Garratt said. "We've got two further warehouses in the town."

With the ability to do smaller maltings come the opportunities to work with single farmers and to match customers with local growers. Garratt refers to them as "warranty crops," which have a warranty of origin.

"We have brewers all around the UK that want their own barley back, and we can do that," he said. "It is a bit of a storage and logistical challenge, but that is a real unique opportunity that small maltsters have."

The flexibility built into the maltings also allows Warminster to produce a wide variety of different malts, a significant advantage in what Garratt calls "a world where brewers want an individual malt for each of their individual beers.

"When my career started 43 years ago, we would make generic malts and the brewer may buy four of them and therefore have the ability to blend his malts and make all his beers. Brewers don't want to do that now. They want to buy multiple malts from me," with fine gradations between them, such as a very light ale malt and a pilsner malt that may be different by one degree Lovibond.

Warminster has also learned how to manage rye and wheat production. The rye goes largely to distillers in the United States, but England has seen an uptick in craft distilling recently. "In the last 10 years, whiskey has come down from Scotland to meet us, so there's now a new breed of English whiskey distilleries," he said.

As the industry changes, some things will stay the same. Floor malting will continue to be a hands-on process with variation built in. "Each batch is going to be different," Garratt said. "Everything we do is just on my personal opinion and the skill and experience of the maltsters. Because it's going to take days for the malt to progress, you actually only have to make major decisions once a day. And then live with it because the grain movements will happen, and you can't change it then until the next day.

"It's all hand/eye experience, touching, sniffing, scratching, rubbing. And for that reason, it's very important for me to walk around every day."

Chapter Twelve

Michigan Malt

Wendell Banks is a multitalented, multi-hyphenated craftsman who began malting when there was very little concept of local malt production.

A farmer-maltster-brewer-distiller, Banks was one of the first craft maltsters in the United States. After malting a batch of barley — about 20 bags' worth — while running the Mountain Town Station brewery in Mt. Pleasant, Michigan, in the late '90s, Banks set off on his own to open Michigan Malt in Shepherd. He estimates that he operated for about 15 years before closing his doors in 2017, while Dave Thomas in *The Craft Maltsters' Handbook* puts the opening of Michigan Malt in 2000.

"I had never grown grain before," Banks said. "I was literally doing this by myself with nothing in front of me. I did it for 10 or 15 years with no one else getting interested, and then it exploded." Prior to brewing, he was farming, growing organic vegetables, and early on received a grant from the state to plant barley. The following year, he received a USDA grant to grow barley and hops and to go to Europe for a month to visit malthouses in Slovakia and the Czech Republic.

There was a long history of growing barley for Stroh's Brewery in the Michigan "thumb," where the rich soil and cool air off of Lake Huron mitigate the usual heat and humidity, until about 1985. Eventually, though, the vagaries of trying to grow malting barley in Michigan and trying to make a living as a craft maltster became too much. Some years there was a good harvest, but there were also plenty of years with uncooperative weather.

"A minimum bet on barley growing is $30,000. For us it was $60,000, and there's no insurance for it," he said. Banks is a big believer in malting barley as the end user, advocating in favor of a 500-pound uni-malter that's "not much larger than your kitchen table," but he advises caution for those looking to malt in areas where barley may not thrive.

"The best reason to be a maltster is because you own a distillery," he said. "Distilling is forgiving. If your barley is a disaster, you can get enzymes. You may not get good single malt out of it, but you can at least put it through a column and make vodka with it. Instead of losing $60,000, we can turn it into $120,000."

Banks built his malt equipment, a roughly two-ton system, based on a bean drier, with a running gear, a hoist and a wedge-wire bottom. He originally operated it as a uni-malter, but pretty quickly learned that if he took the malt out and spread it on the floor after steeping, he could increase his throughput dramatically by freeing up his equipment for steeping or kilning.

"The logjam is germination," he said. "If you take it out and put it on the floor and free it up, you double capacity." Eventually he added a separate steeping tank and brought a system that had originally produced 20 tons a year up to an annual production of 55 tons.

Banks said his method for malting was intuitive, "It's based on repetition and experience," He said malting Is "a discipline of repetition. We dial in our process, and repeat and repeat and repeat, and make small adjustments along the way."

Banks didn't rely on any lab equipment in his facility, an old barn. "I'm a right-brain person," he said. "The thing that I really enjoyed about the way I did it, it's the alchemy, it's the sorcery. It's not science or engineering, it's being in touch with the elements. The temperature today, humidity. I enjoyed manipulating the elements. To be a part of it, it was spiritual. That approach is really not how they're teaching it."

He is reminded of breweries that have "plug-and-play" equipment. "It doesn't mean you're a brewer, it just means you had $200,000 to spend," Banks said. "If I come into your brewery, and you've built all your equipment out of repurposed stainless steel and dairy equipment, I assume that I'm going to drink phenomenal beer. Because you know the process well enough not only to get through the brewing process, but enough to build the damn thing."

He malted during the traditional seasons, using the weather in his favor during the fall, winter and part of the spring. He would load 3,500 pounds of barley, lose about 20 percent of that weight to respiration and see additional losses at cleaning and packing before finishing with 2,500 pounds of malt.

He didn't have a particular target steep temperature or regimen, but played it by ear. A steeping schedule might look like a four-hour soak, an eight-hour air rest, an eight-hour steep, another eight-hour air rest, and a six- to eight-hour final steep. He would look for chitting, the very beginning of growth, before casting the malt. "That means that it's hydrated," he said.

He would do steeping tests in Mason jars every time he got a new batch of grain, steeping samples for two, four and eight hours. One of the biggest issues he would see is water sensitivity, when the water races into the barley and overhydrates it.

"The most critical part of malting is steeping," Banks said. "You don't want to drown the babies, all you want to do in the first steep is to give it a little drink. Each time you hydrate it, the water enters the grain more easily." Once he had cast the green malt, he would turn it every 12 hours to release CO_2, using everything from rakes, a pitchfork, a rototiller and even his feet. "I find the easiest way is if you have a dedicated pair of rubber boots. I would just put my feet next to each other and shimmy up and down the rows," he said.

At 24 hours he would start to see rootlets, and on day two he would start splitting the kernels open to look for the sprout. His preferred measure to gauge full modification is the acrospire length, looking for 90% of them at three-quarters to the full length of the grain. "It never works that evenly, a few percent will be fast," he said.

Once he was ready to dry the malt, he would load it back into the uni-malter at 16 to 18 inches deep and hook up his blower/heater for six to eight hours. He would run it at low temperature until the free moisture was driven off. "It should be past gummy, chewy. You should be getting back to structure in the grain," he said. Then he would turn up the heat.

Using an "unorthodox" approach, he didn't have a variable-speed fan. "The way I did it was totally unteachable and undesirable," Banks said. "I had a fan that was big enough to power six of the units it was powering. You could hear it a half-mile away."

Seth Klann, right, talks to a group of brewers visiting Mecca Grade Estate Malt, while the visitors take turns looking inside the mechanical floor malter.

Chapter Thirteen

Mecca Grade Estate Malt

If technology is able to bring floor malting into the 21st century, it may look something like Mecca Grade Estate Malt.

Armed with a custom-built, all-in-one malting machine, the Madras, Oregon, farm goes back to the beginning of the 20th century, but Mecca Grade's approach is as modern as floor malting gets, eliminating a good deal of the handling and moving of grain and green malt. The centerpiece of their malting operation, the mechanical floor malter steeps, turns and kilns the malt in an enclosed, climate-controlled environment.

"We didn't want to have a bunch of people shoveling," Brad Klann said. "We wanted to get rid of a lot of the labor. There's still a lot of labor. Not as much as the old way. We didn't want to have to move from vessel to vessel or compartment to compartment."

With a couple of conveyor belts, irrigators, air-conditioning, air injection and venting and three propane burners, it's most of a malthouse in one big steel box. Brad and his son, Seth, worked with engineers to have a prototype built that could handle 700 pounds of grain, then scaled up to the current batch size: 12 to 13 tons. It's an automated rig in some ways, with temperature and humidity sensors built in, but it's only as good as the operator. "No matter how computerized you get it, you've got to have somebody who's competent," Brad Klann said.

It's a modern touch for a family that traces its farming roots back to the 1700s, when the abolitionist Luelling family left their North

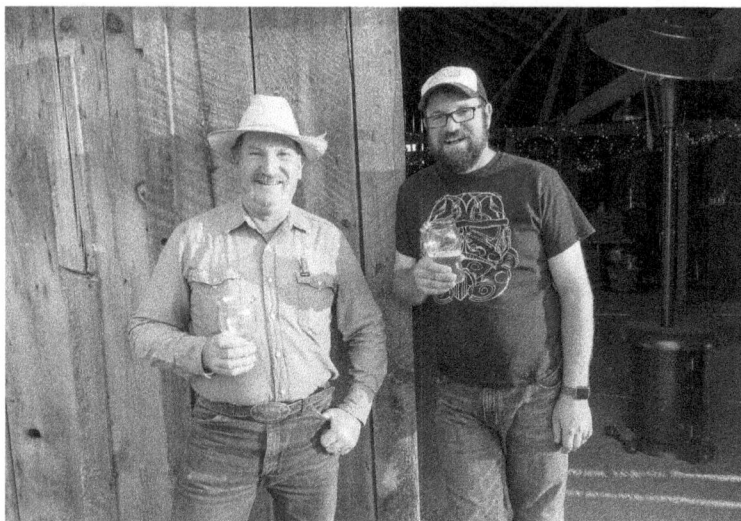

Father and son, farmers and maltsters: Brad and Seth Klann enjoy a beer made from specialty barley grown and malted at Mecca Grade Estate Malts, in Madras, OR.

Carolina farm, settling first in Iowa and later moving on to Oregon, where Henderson Luelling planted the parent stock to most of the Willamette Valley's orchards. His grandson, Seth Luelling, left the nursery with his wife, Cora, and they settled down in Madras in 1904 to establish the farm under the Homestead Act, building the barn and the original house (where Brad's son, Seth, and his family now live) after the winter of 1905.

The family dry-farmed the property, which averaged about 15 inches of rain a year, but the area was hit by a drought that lasted several years and turned central Oregon into a ghost town.

"When that hit, my great-grandpa (Seth Luelling) started a freight business, lumber and grain, raised chickens and livestock. They were able to hang on," Klann said. The graphic of a man on a horse-drawn cart they use on malt bags and promotional material is based on a photo of Luelling taking a load of grain down the Mecca Grade, three miles and 900 vertical feet down to the Deschutes

River, where the railroad used to come through the town of Mecca. Several now vanished towns from around the area — Pelton, Lamonta, Vanora — have been memorialized as the names of their different products.

Irrigation came to the area in 1948 or 1949, and one uncle sold off his 240 acres. Klann bought it back a few years ago, as well as another 320-acre family parcel and a few smaller pieces, eventually rounding it out to 1,000 acres of mostly Kentucky bluegrass for lawn seed.

After Seth came back from college and started homebrewing — and buying malt — they looked at growing malting barley, given that they plant grass seed for four years, then rotate it out with a grain crop for a year or two. The premium for quality barley or wheat wasn't great, so they decided to look at malting their own.

The Klann's watch a total solar eclipse from the top of their four one-million pound grain silos at Mecca Grade Estate Malt.

"Seth started out with a little five-gallon bucket. Then he went up to a cement mixer and was malting in that and spraying water in there, and had a little refrigerator he turned into a kiln," Klann said. It was successful enough to build the prototype and plug away for a year or two, supplying The Ale Apothecary in Bend and Mad Fritz Beer in the Napa Valley. Seth, who had studied graphic arts at Oregon State, did the design work for the Mecca Grade brand and they started building the full-size malting machine. To supply it, they have four one-million-pound silos on-site, as well as smaller ones on adjacent properties.

With an eye on creating a premium product through consistent germination and malting, they screen the grain thoroughly prior to putting it in to malt. The small kernels get mixed with the rootlets and some molasses and sold as deer feed. The cleaned grain goes into one-ton boxes that are forklifted up to the uni-malter, and the forks rotate down to dump the grain in.

Once inside the uni-malter, the grain goes through a one-of-a-kind hydration program. Rather than an immersion steep, it gets constantly turned over and sprayed, raising the grain from eight percent moisture to 45% over a 36–48 hour period. The spray water drains through the grain and flows to on-site storage for use as irrigation water.

The grain germinates for three and a half to six days. They maintain a moisture level of 45% using the sprayers and hold the temperature between 60–65°F. The grain, which swells to a depth of 14 inches, is slowly turned on the conveyor system, with a complete turning achieved every six hours.

Once the green malt is ready, they'll turn on the burners and occasionally rotate the malt to make sure it dries evenly, with temperatures of 130°F or lower. The grain continues to be turned through kilning, with the speed increasing slightly as they reach the final kiln temperature. This allows them to get the malt kilned consistently through the bed, avoiding what Klann called the "salt and pepper look" of malt from a big producer that has been dried in a deep bed.

"When you've got an eight-foot or six-foot bed, you've got stratification there when you start kilning," resulting in varied color levels at different places in the bed, Klann said. "Well, we hit our numbers. Exactly." Their malt will sit and mellow for a couple of days after malting, since the flavor profile tends to be more intense as it comes out of the machine. Finished malt passes through a deculmer and seed cleaner, then a 50-pound bag filler.

The malting equipment is automated and programmable; they primarily use grain-bed temperature and air temperature to drive heating and cooling, but they're constantly checking on progress, measuring grain-bed moisture several times a day and at specific points in the kilning process. They determine whether a malt is finished based on quick-color methods using a spectrophotometer, and by taste.

Mecca Grade has revived Full Pint, an older strain of barley developed by Oregon State University and since picked up by Great Western Malting. It's a more flavorful but less agronomically desirable variety that didn't work for commodity maltsters.

Because Full Pint is a publicly available variety, Mecca Grade is also funding the Next Pint Project to develop new varieties of malting barley with OSU, crossing Full Pint and several other varieties, starting with 130 different crosses planted on their farm in 2016. The selected varieties will become proprietary to Mecca Grade, but all non-selected varieties and information will be available to the public for further breeding projects. As of late 2018, the strains had been whittled down to five proprietary varieties, three of which would be micro-malted, brewed into pale ale and put before commercial sensory panels at the university. They'll then settle on a single variety to cultivate on the farm.

They built the facility to fit four malting machines, but Klann now thinks they'll install only three. Mecca Grade sends off samples of each batch to Hartwick College for full analysis, but they have a 2.5-gallon PicoBrew and a half-barrel HERMS brewhouse and a well-stocked lab setup, including the moisture meter and spectrophotometer, friabilimeter, CO_2 meters and thermometer. They use a magnetic, heated stir plate for congress mashes, which can provide information such as extract and color.

Most importantly, they have a good story and a good product.

"We're providing something that not a lot of people can do," he said. Beyond that, "We've been here a long time. Been through it all. We're about the oldest family out here."

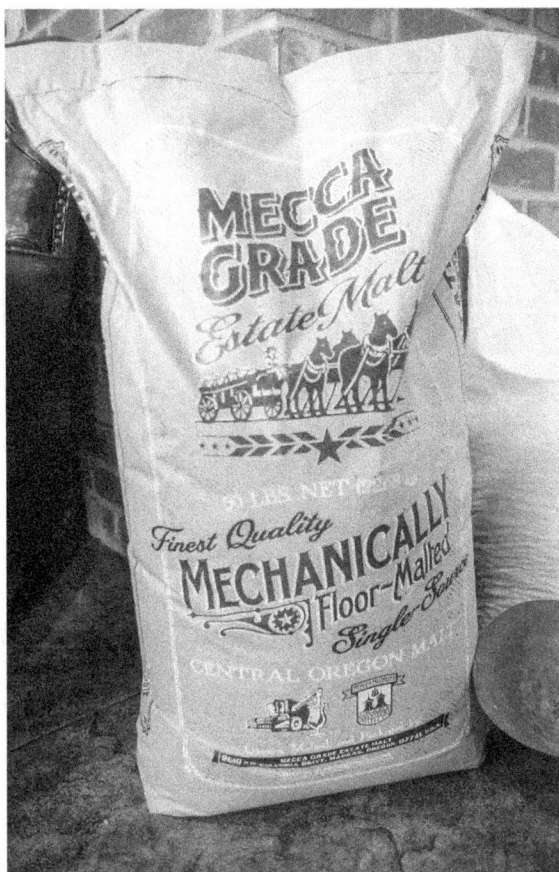

The Mecca Grade Estate Malt bag features a graphic based on an old photograph of Seth Luelling, taking a load of grain to market.

Deer Creek Malthouse, Glen Mills, PA

Chapter Fourteen

Deer Creek Malthouse

Deer Creek Malthouse may be a craft malthouse, but it's also a rustic, old, family farm at heart.

Located in a renovated 150-year-old barn outside of Philadelphia, Deer Creek owner Mark Brault describes his malting as "very small and experimental in nature. All of our equipment is made from reclaimed or recycled farm equipment: steep tank made from a salvage yard scrap steel mixing tank, kiln made from a shipping container and a deculmer made from an old corn sheller," he said. "It's a very simple, manual-intensive process, but very effective at making consistent, high-quality, flavorful malt."

He began trying to make malt in 2012, planting malting barley that year on the farm, malting pilot batches in his basement and brewing with it at home. As he learned more about the process and the industry, he saw "a disconnect in the regional supply chain." While craft distilleries and breweries were popping up all across the mid-Atlantic, there was no local malt supply to link the brewers and local farmers.

"Pennsylvania has a rich history of agriculture," he said, "and there seemed like an opportunity to add value to local grain and help brewers, distillers and food artisans innovate by supplying high-quality, flavorful, malt ingredients that were more aligned with some of their needs," he said. He became passionate about the effort to de-commoditize malt and opened the first post-Prohibition commercial malting in the state. Brault said that the labor- and space-intensive aspects of floor malting, while being able to

Top—A rake and a bed of grain sit on the malting floor at Deer Creek Malthouse, Glen Mills, PA.

Bottom—Sacks of grain at Deer Creek Malthouse

make high-caliber malt, outweighed the upsides of pneumatic malting. It also allows him to experiment without risking an entire full-size batch.

"Of course, floor malting is romantic and marketable since we're located on a farm, and it pays homage to the traditional methods," he said. "It is impossible to achieve the same level of consistency from top to bottom of a grain bed during germination with a four-foot bed of grain versus a four-inch bed of grain."

He malts batches as small as 20 pounds and as big as 3,000 pounds, making a variety of malt ingredients for both food and beverage producers. Some of his malt is estate-grown, while the rest is single-origin grain contracted from other farmers in the region. Early on, he spent a great deal of time looking at the agronomic and malting characteristics of different strains of barley, growing test plots of up to 70 varieties in a year, and at Deer Creek they continue to learn more about the grain-quality attributes that factor into malting quality.

"This has always been and continues to be an area of ongoing improvement and importance to us," he said. "The entire value proposition — not just the economics — needs to make sense for the farmer, maltster, brewer/distiller, distributor and retailer if applicable, and the end consumer. This is hard to do on a small scale."

Brault runs a roughly seven-day batch cycle, sometimes longer, depending on grain type, malt type or growing season, with a slow, low-temperature germination of 54–56°F. A high steep-out moisture, sometimes greater than 46%, avoids watering on the floor and reduces vegetative growth near the end of germination. He turns the malt every six to eight hours. He also malts some older European varieties, with lower enzyme levels and higher beta-glucan, which need added care to shepherd them through malting.

In addition, because of rain, the variability of grain grown on the Eastern Seaboard can make malting even more difficult.

To help them deal with those challenges, Deer Creek does lab-scale testing on new varieties or when conditions change. If they need to improvise on the germination floor, they can adjust the room heating, humidity, turning frequency or germination time.

"Although we have a way to heat the water in the winter, we do not have an easy way to cool it in the summer," Brault said. "Instead of using a chiller, we simply reduce steep duration in the summer to prevent over-hydration, which can lead to uncontrolled growth during germination, or in the case of water-sensitive barley, loss of embryo viability."

As well as test-maltings, Deer Creek performs a variety of in-house and off-site lab testing, including full-spectrum testing that includes protein, DON and enzyme package. When it comes to release-testing a batch of finished malt, Brault said he's looking to answer two questions: Did they make malt? And: How do they characterize the malt so that an end user will know how to use it? To determine question one, they look at key indicators, such as the ratio of soluble to total protein, beta-glucans, friability and enzyme content.

The second question requires looking at characteristics that are consequences of modification and relate to how the ingredient will perform in the brewhouse, distillery or kitchen. These factors include potential extract, pH, color, viscosity, filtration time and fermentability. Depending on the intended usage, some factors will be more or less important, such as kernel size (more important for brewers with a roller mill, less important for a distiller using a hammer mill or a baker using a stone mill).

Flavor also falls into category two, but is more complex, Brault said, so he has standardized methods, scoring and verbiage, as well as a sensory panel to qualitatively and quantitatively characterize malt flavor and aroma. For some malt analyses, they have set control limits and specifications, while for others they are still trying to understand and develop the proper specifications. "In the meantime," he said, "we do the best we can to characterize every malt ingredient transparently, so the end user is empowered to make purchasing decisions and devise recipes."

Resources

BOOKS

Malts and Malting, Dennis E. Briggs (Springer, 1998).

Craft Maltsters Guild *Quality & Safety Manual* (Craft Maltsters Guild, 2017).

Malt: A Practical Guide from Field to Brewhouse, John Mallett (Brewers Publications, 2014).

The Craft Maltsters' Handbook, Dave Thomas (White Mule Press, 2014).

PROFESSIONAL ASSOCIATIONS

Craft Maltsters Guild (https://craftmalting.com) Membership includes access to a network of craft maltsters and a growing library of educational opportunities, such as the annual Craft Malt Conference, and content — not least a series of members-only videos on a variety of topics, from analytical methods to production methods to equipment selection.

American Malting Barley Association (ambainc.org) AMBA is a national organization of large and small maltsters, growers and end users. It furnishes a variety of educational materials on the AMBA website, provides standards for malting barley, funds barley research and organizes the National Barley Improvement Committee.

American Society of Brewing Chemists (https://www.asbcnet.org) Membership provides access to ASBC methods for malt analysis lab procedures, as well as a variety of educational and reference materials.

www.ingramcontent.com/pod-product-compliance
Lightning Source LLC
Chambersburg PA
CBHW060751100426
42813CB00004B/779